HISTORY AND NATIONAL LIFE

PETER MANDLER

HISTORY AND NATIONAL LIFE

P

PROFILE BOOKS

First published in Great Britain in 2002 by
Profile Books Ltd
58A Hatton Garden
London ECIN 8LX
www.profilebooks.co.uk

Typeset in Minion by MacGuru
info@macguru.org.uk

Printed and bound in Great Britain by
Clays, Bungay, Suffolk

A CIP catalogue record for this book is available from the
British Library.

ISBN 1 86197 469 8

CONTENTS

ILLUSTRATIONS

THE HISTORY ROOM

I

THE HISTORY BOOM

Is history the new rock 'n' roll? Journalistic assurances to this effect are perhaps a bit too glib to be taken at face value; after all, only last week the new rock 'n' roll was poetry, the week before that, opera. Nevertheless, gradually over the past generation, and more obviously over the past decade, history seems to have infiltrated the contemporary consciousness at too many levels for it to be ignored. In particular, the hitherto unspeakable tragedies of the first half of the twentieth century – the world wars, the genocides, the awful dawning of the nuclear age – have voiced their demands upon our culture with increasing insistence since the 1960s, as the contrasts deepen between the horrors witnessed by the older generation and the comparatively uneventful lives of the young. Booker Prize winners loot early twentieth-century history for settings and characters and problematics. Documentarists make grim use of the fact that the events of the early twentieth century are the first to have been fully recorded in audio and video, latterly in colour. As the survivors die off, historians discover a new role – helping society to do its 'memory work', preserving its fading traces in print as well as in monument and museum. The gravity of the horrors is thought to have made remembering the past a moral imperative, in ways it had not always been before. Remembering is something the dead demand of us, like medieval nobles leaving funds for requiem masses in eternity; but it seems at the same time to offer immediate uses, lessons for practical application.

It is not only world war and genocide that has made us want to – or feel we ought to – remember. We also now, on an unprecedented scale, seek to reach out to our ancestors, near and far. The internet makes it easier to reunite families across the generations, as it reunites friends in the present. When the Americans opened their Ellis Island website in April 2001, 50 million users sought to gain access on the first day. When the Public Record Office tried to launch the 1901 census on line in January 2002, 29 million users a day logged on in the first four days and threatened to bring down the entire British telephone network. But even without the internet, the record offices have been filling up for years with genealogists and family historians. As physical traces of family are erased by social and geographical mobility, more and more people seek to create a virtual family projected backwards in historical time – sometimes very far backwards. DNA testing can nominally affiliate you to one of seven 'tribes' descended from one of seven prehistoric ancestors, or, more plausibly, find people in Devon directly descended from prehistoric Devonians whose DNA has been extracted from excavated bones. Television archaeologists invite you to 'meet your ancestors'. Perhaps even these very remote ancestors provide a more individualised form of identity, better suited to a highly individualised society than the traditional markers of identity, class, religion or nation.

But, then, the contemporary lust for history is not only about remembering – for some of those nominal ancestors are pretty remote indeed, and the fascination with the reconstructed Roman legionnaire from the archaeological site surely goes beyond the demand for a personal connection. History also offers the charm of the exotic – something almost completely out of reach, as the Himalayas and the South Seas are no longer. Recent bestsellers in Britain include not only tales of familiar English heroes and biographies of the already celebrated English queens and kings, but also portraits of hitherto obscure eighteenth-century noblewomen, or the discoverers of longitude and the dye that gave us mauve. Popular television series venture further afield still, following in the steps of Alexander and the Aztecs. Simon Schama's celebrity, now firmly associated with a drum-and-trumpet version of Britain's national history, was in fact founded upon plunges into the stranger soil of seventeenth-century Holland. While computer graphics have until now been applied principally to the creation of almost unimaginable worlds – futuristic ones and prehistoric ones – where primitive techniques of realisation are safer from criticism, it seems highly likely that they will soon move on to almost imaginable worlds from history, further fuelling the public's appetite. While all of these popular histories gain in interest by playing on the tension between the familiarity of universal humanity and the oddity of lost worlds, they are not about 'memory' or 'identity' in any straightforward sense.

The purpose of this short book is to sort out these multiple uses of history, to show when and why they have arisen separately, even as today they seem to flow together, and finally to suggest which uses of history the work of the professional historian can appropriately support. History is so ubiquitous, and has so many different audiences and uses, that attempts to articulate its purpose tend either to lump together incompatible goals or to collapse into incoherent generalities. Nor do the purposes of history that lay people cite correspond very well to those articulated (on those rare occasions when they articulate them at all) by professional historians in universities. If you ask first-year history undergraduates today why they are studying history – what use is it to them – they respond almost universally in two ways. History teaches lessons, they say – by which they mean, mostly, moral or at best political lessons derived from the first half of the twentieth century: how international understanding might prevent war; how racial tolerance might protect minorities from genocidal furies; how restraint upon the hubris of science might avert environmental nightmares. Alternatively, they say, history tells us who we are – that is, it provides an identity which we can no longer get from oral tradition or continuity of experience.

Yet neither of these rationales is very satisfying to the professional historian, nor, in reality, do they have much to do with the history people are consuming.

As for the lessons that history teaches, most historians, especially those who are educators, *would* want to argue that history teaches lessons – but they would not reach for those very immediate and obvious lessons that students have in mind. You do not need history, surely, to argue for international dialogue or racial tolerance or nuclear arms control; and if you do, your broken moral compass is bound eventually to overrule any book learning. Furthermore, as it should go without saying, history is no laboratory; it offers fewer opportunities for the testing of hypotheses than even the social sciences, which have not been conspicuously successful in teaching lessons in recent years. The kinds of lessons history can teach are abstract, so abstract, in fact, that we ought not to call them lessons at all; they lie among the kinds of human enrichment that we look to all the arts to provide, although history, because of its uniquely wide range of subject matter and approaches, has better claims as a provider of these riches than many other humanistic disciplines. Historians like to say that history is the queen of the humanities.

To an extent, historians have been complicit in the popular misperception of the educational value of history. It is terribly tempting to claim some higher consciousness of the underlying processes in the middle of, or immediately after, epochal events like wars or revolutions (especially if they go wrong) – claims of this kind were widely made in the 1920s and 1930s, and again, though less often, in the 1950s and 1960s. Military historians are still much in demand for lecturing on strategy and tactics at officer training colleges, which may account for the tendency among generals always to be fighting again the *last* war. (Admittedly, military campaigns do offer something more like laboratory conditions than other historical scenarios.) Few historians make such claims any longer. The yearning for history to teach lessons is more likely to arise now on the demand side, as ordinary citizens recoil from the horrors of the recent past and seek some reassurance from historians that they need not recur. But that, I think, is properly part of the honouring and memorialising side of the recent history boom, which is not a part to which historians can legitimately contribute a great deal.

As for the notion that history tells us who we are, historians have been much more than complicit with the idea of history as an underpinning for national identity – for they know that the whole evolution of their discipline has been tied up with that idea. At the same time, they know that their discipline – and their audience – has for long been outgrowing that idea. There *are* still a small number who feel, with David Starkey, that if 'we do not believe in nation' then 'we do not believe in history', that 'you cannot have history without nationhood',[1] and – as we shall see – they have disproportionate influence because few other historians have yet offered alternative reasons to believe in history. But good manners alone suggests to those who write on recent British history, as I do, that the historical profession as a whole can hardly be justified by reference to that portion that clearly relates to twenty-first century British identity. More seriously, if we dismiss all history that does not subserve national identity, then we are dismissing most of the history that people are consuming today – including those kinds of history that provide material for identities that are non-national – local, familial, sexual, professional or aesthetic and stylistic identities, to name a few. Arguably, too, an excessive consciousness of history can distort as much as bolster national identity – by laying too much stress on elements of continuity at the expense of change, for example.

Why have historians been so slow to propose alternative rationales? As Starkey points out, for much of the last century the growth of the university has provided them with a captive audience of students and fellow academics who require no rationale: the forward momentum of professionalisation and specialisation has provided quite enough impetus. There is a lot of truth to this explanation, and it has been given one last push by the great expansion of higher education in Britain in the last decade, which has seen the proportion of 20-year-olds in higher education more than double. The captive audience which has thus recently expanded requires servicing with a raft of textbooks which tell them *how* to do history without necessarily telling them *why*. This tendency for historians writing about their craft to dwell upon method at the expense of purpose has been further aggravated by a methodological attack on historians from within the academic world, from 'postmodernists' (principally in literature departments) who have made a frontal assault on history precisely by questioning its methods rather than its social function. For example, to take only the two best books in the recent flood of general books about history, Richard Evans's *In Defence of History* (1997) is much more of a polemic about historical method than the justification for the whole enterprise that the title suggests, while Ludmilla Jordanova's *History In Practice* (2000) is, as its title does suggest, a quasi-anthropological account of how history is practised which takes the existence of serious historical research more or less for granted.

Taking history for granted is no longer an option, if only because the captive audience is no longer captive. The assumption that history's place in the university is naturally and forever secured might have been safe in the early years of higher education when the nationalist rationale was still a trump card, but its purchase has diminished as nationalism has run into the sand and the range of higher education options has extended. Nowadays it is quite common for academic historians to puzzle over the hard times history is allegedly experiencing in higher education, while in the mass media history booms – but this only points up how unaccustomed historians are to having to argue their corner. There are legitimate connections to be made between the uses of history and the appeal history makes to the mass market, but they need to be drawn, and separated from those illegitimate connections – nationalist and utilitarian – about which most historians today feel either guilty or irritated.

Today we live still very much under the shadow of the nationalist origins of history. Rather like anthropologists, whose morale has been badly sapped by the guilty consciousness of the racial and imperial origins of their discipline, historians shy away from considering the uses of their discipline for fear of stirring up dying chauvinist embers. But they will need to mobilise all of their best arguments if they are to benefit fully from today's history boom. As the chapters that follow will suggest, while the popular audience for history arose initially from the nationalist fervour of the nineteenth century, in the twentieth century it seemed possible that the dying away of nationalism might lead also to the fading of popular appetites for history. The unprecedented history boom from the 1960s onwards has dispelled those fears. If historians are to take advantage of the unparalleled opportunities offered by this boom, they must transcend the nationalist origins of their discipline and chart a new social purpose for history in the twenty-first century.

II

NATIONALIST ORIGINS

1800–1880

Before the French Revolution, history neither needed nor wanted a popular audience. In the eighteenth century it had only just pulled itself out of various kinds of disrepute among the 'polite'. Antiquarians had given it a 'dry as dust' reputation by accumulating and luxuriating in pointless piles of disconnected facts. Political and religious controversialists had polluted it with bias and venom in pursuing their chosen vendettas. Polite historians strained to detach their work from these associations. They cultivated a lighter, more refined style; presented their work in large, formal and expensive volumes, often available only by subscription; disclaimed any immediate political or religious usefulness. They were aiming to complement, or substitute for the cultivating qualities traditionally attached to the classics, an ambition for which they had classical backing. Livy had called history 'the best medicine for a sick mind; for in history you have a record of the infinite variety of human experience plainly set out for all to see'. Polybius had said that history was 'the best school wherein a man may learn how to conduct himself in all the situations of life', Dionysius of Halicarnassus that 'history is philosophy teaching by examples'. The suspicion lingered that modern historians could never quite match the *gravitas* of the classics: their raw material was not sufficiently stirring (hardly surprising, if blanched of past political and religious unpleasantness), their philosophy never very profound. The scholar statesman Bolingbroke said in the early eighteenth century that historians made good companions – agreeable, but no more.

The philosophers of the Enlightenment made use of history without ever valuing it very highly in its own right. Mostly they viewed the past as a deep sump of barbarism and error, not without its monitory value – providing a road map of characteristic pitfalls in the progress towards modernity – but not of the same kind of immediate practical value as that yielded by, for example, the direct observation of nature. It was both too lurid and too easy. 'It always takes more pains and application to look into, let us say, the kind of machine that could provide Paris with plenty of water – which we surely need', wrote Voltaire, 'whereas all one has to do in order to learn the old wives' tales handed down to us under the name of history is to open one's eyes and read. These tales are told over and over again, even though they do not much matter to us.'[1] In the right hands, however, the raw stuff of history could be shaped and moulded into those confident trajectories with which the *philosophes* sketched the progression of humanity from the primitive state to modern civilisation.

The French Revolution changed all that, both by failing and by succeeding. Its failure caused a chastened younger generation of *philosophes* to reconsider how thoroughly the progress of civilisation had in fact erased the previous stages of human evolution. Perfectibility was not so evidently imminent; and perhaps those stubbornly persisting flaws in humanity which differentiated classes and peoples were not so contemptible – perhaps, indeed, they were essential, woven into the human fabric either culturally or biologically, needing to be taken into account when drawing up any further blueprints for progress. The idea of the nation and the idea of history thus burgeoned together, symbiotically: each nation had its own path to the future, a path which led from different pasts. These ideas might have remained only that, the possession of a cluster of romantic intellectuals, had the French Revolution not also succeeded – revealing the force of the *levée en masse*, the whole of the people mobilised to fight for the idea of the nation. It may have taken another half century to persuade the crowned heads of Europe, but by the mid-nineteenth century there were few European societies left unmoved by nationalism – among intellectuals, but also among the common people and even the élites.

Most states pretty soon saw the wisdom of arming themselves with national historians who could first define the people along the linguistic, racial, cultural and territorial lines that best suited the State, then inspire them by making them the heroes of their own story, and so spur them on to future acts of glory in the service of their nation. The French got in on the act early; one of the specialities of their first revolution was the collection and display of historical memorials of the *ancien régime*, a gruesome fascination with the crimes of the fallen that gave way strangely but inexorably to appreciation, and ultimately to national pride. The great French romantic historians of the post-Napoleonic period could trace their love affair with the past back to childhood wanderings through Europe's first national history museum, Alexandre Lenoir's *Musée des Monuments Français*, opened in the confiscated Convent of the Augustinians in 1795. They then found jobs in the range of Napoleonic and post-Napoleonic institutions erected to organise the French national archives, preserve the French national monuments, and write the French national history. By 1833 even the Palace of Versailles had been transformed into a French historical museum at the behest of its restored royal owner, the Citizen King Louis Philippe.

The German states quickly followed suit, having felt the full brunt of what a mobilised nation could do to its unmobilised neighbours in 1806, when they were humiliated by Napoleon. A German national historical museum was mooted almost immediately after peace broke out in 1815, and the idea eventually crystallised in 1852, in Nuremberg, some two decades before the German nation itself. In the meantime, the multiplicity of German states only multiplied the opportunities to do official history, each in their own way. Professorships of History spread across the German archipelago, kings and princelings 'nationalised' their own archives and historical museums, and entire disciplines were created: *Heimatkunde* (the study of the homeland), *Volkskunde* (the study of the people), *Volksgeschichte* (the history of the people).

New states that had no history (as states) had to invent one. The Belgians, who wriggled out of the grip of foreign rulers for the first time in 1830, were highly creative players of this game, foraging busily around in the past for prehistoric as well as historic forebears. The Italians had an easier time of it, geographically, but in no other way, for their peninsula was extremely diverse in linguistic, cultural and historical terms; every historian of nationalism cites the statistic that at unification in 1860 only 2.5 per cent of the population were fluent speakers of Italian. As was famously said at the time by the Piedmontese minister Massimo

D'Azeglio, 'We have made Italy. Now we have to make Italians.' An artificial history had to be cultivated for this purpose. On the other hand, in the nineteenth century, even the most 'natural' nations whipped up a confected history specifically to serve the new needs of their nation states. It was a Frenchman, Ernest Renan, who defined the nation as a collection of individuals who have some things in common and have chosen to forget – or to remember differently – everything else. To Renan's credit, he added that, as a result, 'progress in historical studies often constitutes a danger for nationality'.[2] In 1882 this was still more a hopeful remark than an accurate one.

It would be a mistake, however, to view the new national history simply as state-sponsored propaganda. For one thing, national history in many places – especially the multi-national empires – had originated as a movement in opposition to the State and was only later co-opted by states for their own purposes. For another, if it had been too wooden and mechanical, it would not have shaped hearts and minds as it was supposed to do. For a third, its artists were themselves true believers. In one of the most celebrated passages of modern French literature, Augustin Thierry, the founder of French romantic history, recounted the moment in 1810 when his historical fire was first lit: he had been reading a tale of early Frankish heroism and was so caught up in the story that he rose from his seat and began marching up and down the room, chanting with the Franks their noble war song. For his great successor, Jules Michelet, the spark was provided by Lenoir's museum of monuments. No one had to pay them to write their national histories; that was an added (and later) bonus.

Their inspiration showed in the style and method of their history, which easily and rightly won a mass audience. Firstly, they made the common people the subjects of their national story: for Thierry, the nation had originated in the independence and valour of the 'communes' in early medieval struggles against the English; for Michelet, the nation was literally the salt of the earth, the peasants who toiled in the fields and whose blood and sweat had fertilised the soil. Secondly, they pitched their prose style judiciously to this new audience, as well. Thierry squeezed the analytical content out of Enlightenment history and sought to let the story speak for itself (carefully arranging the narrative, of course, so that it did so). He condemned modern historians for painting the past in 'uncertain colours' – a telling phrase – and made sure his own colours were bold and full of meaning. Michelet, whose audience a generation later was more plebeian still, absorbed the quasi-religious mysticism and apocalyptic language of his day, investing his history with heightened drama and emotion. Students today reading Thierry and Michelet can hardly comprehend them – history ought not to show off like this, with its heart on its sleeve, and its authors so visible, so vainglorious. But it certainly captured the loyalties of the newly literate masses of Europe in the first great age of nationalism.

But what about the English? It is often held that the English had no nationalism, at least not in the early nineteenth century. Unconquered and indeed undaunted by the French, their élites either did not need to mobilise their masses, or had more traditional ways of doing that. A long history of geographical separation from the rest of Europe, linguistic and religious unity, and continuous, slowly evolving political institutions meant that a kind of 'pre-national' consciousness was already there should the need arise to raise taxes and recruit armies, without having to be souped up into modern nationalism. Because Henry V and Shakespeare had already done the job for 'England', there was no need to make a song and dance about 'the English'. In certain respects, post-French Revolutionary England can be seen to have gone less national in reaction against the enemy. The military and patriotic mobilisations necessary to fight a century of wars against the French before 1815 were dismantled thereafter. Democracy was damned for the foreseeable future; Britain and Hungary would be the last European states to concede universal male suffrage, in 1918. If any new-fangled ideology gripped England after 1815, it was a dour, disciplinary, moralising evangelical religion, which reinstated class divisions and deliberately dampened popular expectations of the political system.

Yet apart from mobilisation from above, the British were exposed to all of the same nationalising forces as Continental peoples, generally with greater intensity. Regional distinctions were erased by the early creation of a national market and a national transport and communications network. By the 1850s Britain had not only the world's first national railway system, but also its first telegraph network and its largest newspaper readership. Its remaining minority languages were either extinguished (in the case of Cornish) or pushed into mountainous redoubts on its far fringes (in the case of Welsh and Scots Gaelic). Now the most highly urbanised society in Europe, its people were packed tightly together, intimately, living increasingly homogeneous lives whether in Nottingham or Glasgow or Belfast or Bristol. Britain did not have the highest literacy rates in Europe – that honour belonged to Prussia, and within the British Isles Scotland was well ahead of England – but it did have the highest living standards and the lowest levels of censorship, so that reading material flowed widely and freely. Despite its low levels of literacy, its people were twice as likely to post letters to each other as those of any other European country. Already by the 1830s something like the modern mass-circulation press had come into being, initially in the form of popular illustrated weeklies like the *Penny Magazine* (with possibly a million readers a week in the early 1830s), then in the 1840s in the form of the famous British Sunday newspapers, and even more so after 1855 when the last newspaper tax was repealed.

All of these forces operated powerfully to thicken the 'imagined community' of the people, to span class, religious and regional divides, to make people feel a corporate existence on a national scale that they had not felt fully before. That national consciousness did manifest itself to some extent as a grassroots political consciousness, as a demand for wider or universal participation and representation in Parliament, leading to a reform of the franchise in 1832 – still limited, but now more uniform across the United Kingdom – and to the Chartist movement for universal male suffrage in the late 1830s and 1840s. But it manifested itself even more clearly and consistently as a demand for cultural enfranchisement, that is, a demand for acknowledgement of the people as a unified body with common traditions, common habits, a common history and a common future – a demand that was less pressing upon the State, but was also more consistent with well-established British ideals of free expression and voluntary action.

Why did this demand for cultural enfranchisement take the form, as it did, very strikingly, in the 1830s and 1840s, of a seemingly insatiable appetite for *English history*? Both the Englishness and the historicism require some explanation.

Had national consciousness been more political, we would certainly have expected it to take a British form, as the chief political institution, Parliament (though not the Church or the Law), was a body purporting to represent the whole of the United Kingdom. Both the 1832 legislation and the Chartist movement did seek, generally, to address the whole of the British Isles. Today historians still puzzle over the ways in which cultural nationalism expressed itself in nineteenth-century Britain, why 'England' and 'Englishness' became synecdochic – the part standing for the whole of Britain. Wales was still shellshocked by the sudden urbanisation and industrialisation of its now-dominant south, mostly stocked by immigrant Englishmen. To some extent Scotland retained its cultural independence, with its own press, religious and legal institutions, and its own sense of self, including its historical self. Yet many nineteenth-century Scots and Welsh were also obviously eager to share in 'Englishness' and to accept its cultural baggage as their own. The Irish stood further apart; the rise of cultural consciousness widened the fissure between them and the British rather than otherwise, with consequences that we still live with today. However, one straightforward explanation for the Englishness of English history is that British history simply did not exist – there had been no Britain before the Union of Scotland with England and Wales in 1707, and no United Kingdom before 1801. If history was to be the outlet for cultural nationalism, it would have to be English or Scottish or Welsh, not British.

Then, why history? As other European peoples had seen, history offered unique advantages to a nation in search of itself. Since élite historians had generally confined themselves to telling a rather refined and abstracted story, with little depth either chronologically or socially, the field was open to anyone who was willing to put the people at the centre, making them the heroes of their own story. Romantic history on the model of Thierry and Michelet had a special appeal, too, to a newly literate public: a clear narrative structure, vivid characterisation, plentiful opportunities in a pre-photographic age for imaginative pictorial illustration by means of woodcut or steel engraving. Nor need the effect of popular history be backward-looking, nostalgic – few people had anything to be nostalgic about *circa* 1800. By giving the people a long pedigree of blood and culture, reaching back many centuries, history conveyed to the powerless and disenfranchised a tremendous sense of entitlement and potential for the future. Thierry had certainly intended to galvanise the 'third estate' of his own day, rather cast down by the events of the French Revolution, by recounting tales of their past heroics. 'In those vague and pompous narratives', he wrote of 'the inexact, falsified, and colourless compilations' that had hitherto passed for 'histories of France', 'in which a few privileged personages monopolise the historic stage while the mass of the whole nation is hidden behind the mantles of the courtiers, we find neither serious instruction, nor any lessons applicable to ourselves, nor that sympathy which in general interests men in the fate of those who resemble them'.[3] His was decidedly a history for the present and for the future, giving 'new life' to 'the most numerous and most forgotten class of our nation'. Such exhortations, such lessons, were perhaps even more relevant to an English people denied realisation of their collective existence through the motors of politics.

As it happens, the English were not behindhand in devising a popular, romantic history, although, because it came first out of the cultural marketplace rather than the State or the academy, it took the form not of the textbook but of the novel. Thierry's acknowledged master, upon whose style and method he closely modelled his own, was the author of those great fictional epics of English history, *Ivanhoe* (1819) and *Kenilworth* (1821). It is a measure of the complexity of the British phenomenon that this author should be, of course, a Scottish conservative, Walter Scott. Scott provided the makings of *both* Scottish *and* English romantic history, inaugurating the former with the Waverley sequence that began in 1814, but quickly reaching out to the much larger English market with distinctively English settings and themes – for example, the Saxon racial virtues of the English, struggling against their Norman conquerors in *Ivanhoe*, which had such an impact on Thierry. In his heart of hearts, Scott was a true child of the Enlightenment, and scholars analysing his underlying patterns of thought affiliate him to the Scottish Enlightenment's vision of progress from a barbaric past to a modern, polite, commercial society. But he was also a canny commercial writer who knew how to bring the past alive in order to capture the popular imagination. He played deliberately on the tension between the familiar and the strange, situating his stories in well-known landscapes, re-animating ruined or deserted castles and manor houses, summoning up stereotypical folk and rural 'characters' and projecting them centuries backwards to give the reader a sense of both connection and distance. As early as 1802, he was revealing bits of his mature technique to the poet Anna Seward, in explaining one of his ballads: 'Tell a peasant an ordinary tale of robbery and murder, and perhaps you may fail to interest him; but to excite his terrors, you assure him that it happened on the very heath he usually crosses, or to a man whose family he has known.'[4] The technique was novel; even more novel was the hint that such a technique might arouse the interest of a peasant.

Among Scott's strategies was a wide-ranging forage among diverse historical periods to broaden appeal and audience, from eighteenth-century Scotland back to the early middle ages. He hit a rich seam in the early 1820s with a string of novels set in the sixteenth century, of which *Kenilworth* was the most popular with his English audience, and from here forwards we can trace a rising English passion for what came to be known as 'the merry England of Good Queen Bess', or, more loosely, 'England in the Olden Time'. England in the Olden Time provided the perfect pedigree for the burgeoning English reading class of the early nineteenth century: unlike pre-Reformation pasts, it was Protestant, enterprising, commercial, in some respects also imperial; it could plausibly be portrayed as a period of rising living standards for the masses, a time when the sturdy independent yeoman came into his own, able to stand up to (without necessarily defying) his noble and royal betters. The Olden Time had special attractions, too, to readers and writers as the seed bed of a democratic English literature, of Shakespeare and Milton and (stretching the point a little) John Bunyan.

The fashion set by Scott spread rapidly. His own works sold spectacularly: the full sets of the Waverley novels offered by Cadell from 1829 sold in the tens of thousands, and the 'People's Edition', published in parts from 1844, sold *7 million* weekly numbers. They were then copied, pirated, plagiarised, adapted, staged, set to music, drawn, painted, sculpted and monumentalised in public and

private architecture across the map of Europe. The inno-
vation of Scott's historical style with its broad popular
appeal coincided with a technological revolution in print-
ing and, as Stephen Bann has shown, in visual representation, too, so his stories passed through a whole series of
new mass-marketed cultural products: the panorama and
the diorama, the gas-lit theatrical spectacle, the popular illustrated magazine, the framed engraving of a 'fine art'
picture, the penny novel and the serialised saga issued in
parts.

Popular demand, manifested through these new media,
also pressed on the traditional theatres of 'high culture'. In
1821 the painter Charles Leslie was already successfully plotting his breakthrough into the mass market by deliberately
devising a grand history painting with an eye not so much
to the Royal Academy audience as to the engraving market.
Describing what became 'May Day Revels in the Time of
Queen Elizabeth' to his sister, Leslie expressed the hope that
'it will be popular, as it is a period that Englishmen are fond
of recurring to, as one of the most brilliant in the history of
their country. They are also more generally acquainted with
the manners of that time than any other, on account of the
greater popularity of Shakespeare than any other English
writer whatever.'[5] It was a success with the print buyers and
with the Royal Academy, and with Walter Scott, too, who
came to admire it while Leslie was working on it and

induced the artist to add a few archers to heighten the effect. By the 1830s, the popularity of such pictures was bringing the Royal Academy itself into the public eye in a way it had not previously imagined or courted; the peak mid-Victorian years of the R. A. Summer Exhibitions, when literally hundreds of thousands of people pressed through the galleries in a season, were also the peak years of the history painting.

By the 1840s, it was hard to avoid historical themes, especially those set in the Olden Time, in any nook or cranny of high or popular culture. The bestselling author of the day was a man who rather disliked the historical style, Charles Dickens, but he was run a close second by the man who after Scott best personified it, William Harrison Ainsworth. Ainsworth reached his peak of popularity in the 1840s with novels set in real historical monuments of the Olden Time – *The Tower of London, Windsor Castle* and *Old St Paul's*, the latter serialised in the *Sunday Times*, then a well-established but rather low-class popular newspaper. Here Ainsworth was tapping into another new branch of the history industry, popular tourism. Radicals in Parliament had been pressing since the Reform Act of 1832 for wider public access to historical monuments that could reasonably be interpreted as 'national heritage' (though the phrase was not then used): for example, Westminster Abbey, Hampton Court, Windsor Castle and, above all, the

THE

TOWER OF LONDON.

𝔄 𝔥𝔦𝔰𝔱𝔬𝔯𝔦𝔠𝔞𝔩 𝔯𝔬𝔪𝔞𝔫𝔠𝔢.

BY

WILLIAM HARRISON AINSWORTH.

ILLUSTRATED

BY GEORGE CRUIKSHANK.

LONDON:
RICHARD BENTLEY, NEW BURLINGTON STREET,
𝔅𝔬𝔬𝔨𝔰𝔢𝔩𝔩𝔢𝔯 𝔦𝔫 𝔒𝔯𝔡𝔦𝔫𝔞𝔯𝔶 𝔱𝔬 𝔥𝔢𝔯 𝔐𝔞𝔧𝔢𝔰𝔱𝔶.

MDCCCXL.

Title page of Ainsworth's *The Tower of London: A Historical Romance*
(1840)

Tower. Victories had been won; Hampton Court was thrown open for free, and the Tower Armouries re-opened at an affordable 6d. By the 1850s they were drawing hundreds of thousands of visitors annually. Ainsworth wrote *The Tower of London* with an eye to profiting from and further fuelling this tourist market, which is why modern readers puzzle over a text that reads more like a guidebook than a novel – in fact it did double duty.

At this stage many layers of historical consciousness had been built up, with subtly different meanings and audiences, cross-cutting and intermingling. The popular fascination with the Olden Time drew on cultural nationalism, the staking of a claim to cultural democracy by masses newly enfranchised by literacy and new media. In the campaigns for public access to historical monuments, a claim was being staked to more than recognition and self-worth: property that had once been the exclusive preserve of the well-born was being semi-nationalised; a sense of 'national heritage' – physical relics of the past preserved for public purposes in the present – was in embryo. But cultural nationalism was not the monopoly of the masses. Some genteel or even aristocratic figures sought to put themselves at the head of the cultural nation, tweaking the popular historical sense in order to harmonise it better with a hierarchical social order. Disraeli's Young England clique of romantic nobles propounded a top-down version of the cult of the Olden Time. Catholics and crypto-Catholics nursed a cult of medieval chivalric Englishness, which in dilute form – especially through the medium of Tennyson – found an ever-widening audience later in the century.

After the Houses of Parliament burnt down in 1834, the competition to reconstruct them prescribed Gothic or Elizabethan styles; had it not coincided with the historical rage of the late 1830s and 1840s, it might not have done so. When cartoons for the historical paintings planned for the parliamentary interiors were put on public display in the summer of 1843, they drew thousands a day. The prescribed themes for the paintings – British history or scenes from Shakespeare, Spenser and Milton – were obviously *à la mode*, and the idea of public access itself was clearly on the model of the Tower or Hampton Court. At about the same time Parliament authorised the building of a Public Record Office, in Chancery Lane, also in the Elizabethan style; one impetus for this was the need to clear the heaps of public records out of the Tower of London, to make way for tourists.

High Churchmen, too, staked a 'national' claim for a revived Church of England, rooted in history and projected visually in a rage for historically correct Gothic architecture. 1839, a potent year for historical consciousness in Britain, saw the founding of both the Oxford Society for Promoting the Study of Gothic Architecture and the

Cambridge Camden Society for 'the study of Ecclesiastical Architecture and the restoration of mutilated architectural remains'. These architectural societies were among the inspirations for a host of local and county archaeological and historical societies that spread around the country in subsequent decades, and also for the British Archaeological Association founded in 1843.

However, we should not rush to the conclusion from this rash of initiatives and foundings – some of very small and fragile societies indeed – that the popular cult of history met with universal approbation from the old cultural élites. The very fact that much of the impulse came from below was suspicious, and the possible connections between cultural nationalism and political nationalism – Chartism, too, made its appearance on the national stage in 1839 – were threatening. Accordingly, the writers of history for polite audiences were not tremendously welcoming. The pages of the élite quarterlies seethed with complaints that the Scott–Ainsworth style was degrading history by fictionalising, popularising and romanticising it – making it too attractive, in short. The *Edinburgh Review*, assessing George L. Craik and Charles Macfarlane's *Pictorial History of England* (1838–41), regretted the potential eclipse of the 'philosophic' by the 'picturesque' style. Rather perversely, it claimed that 'increased reverence for antiquity tends to the neglect of it', by making the past seem strange and irrelevant; 'history ... sinks from the rank of "philosophy teaching by example", into the category of amateurship and *vertu*'.[6] In a thoughtful but highly critical piece of 1847, 'Walter Scott – Has History Gained by His Writings?', *Fraser's Magazine* answered its question firmly in the negative. Scott's familiarising techniques did violence to the past, by imposing nineteenth-century characteristics on the fifteenth century, and 'we are convinced that what are called Young England views have originated in these falsifications of history'. It was the historian's office 'to note and comment on the *differences*, not the resemblances or the peculiarities of successive ages', so as to give 'a full comprehension of national progress and social advance', as for example Hume had demonstrated. But in fact *Fraser's* was also objecting to giving the past any character at all; accuracy would not have been much better than anachronism. All imaginative representations of the past were dangerous. Scott's 'retentiveness of personal peculiarities seems almost to have amounted to disease'.[7]

Such reactions from respectable organs of liberal opinion explain why England has often been regarded as the exception to the European rule, the land without nationalism, and, in this period at least, without nationalist history. At the popular level, however, England had rather more nationalist history, which had built up a nearly insatiable appetite for historical text, image and spectacle. That appetite could have been harnessed to the writing of 'serious' history, in the way that Thierry and Michelet had proposed. It could also, as a few lonely voices – J. M. Kemble, John Stuart Mill, G. H. Lewes – suggested at the time, be harnessed to 'philosophic' history, by accepting and integrating nationalist history into an overarching theory of progress and development. It might even improve the writing of serious history. Thomas Carlyle, indulging one of his favourite pastimes, crying out in the wilderness, proclaimed, 'These historical novels have taught all men this truth, which looks like a truism, yet was unknown to writers of history and others, till so taught: that the bygone ages of the world were actually filled with living men, not by protocols, state papers, controversies and abstractions of men.'[8]

The germ was there; until 1848, at least, it was not developed.

Thomas Babington Macaulay was undoubtedly the most nationally celebrated and most widely read British historian of the nineteenth century, but he represented only a halfway house between philosophic and nationalist history. Coming from the *Edinburgh Review* stable and a career as a Whig MP, he began with ambitions for history that were firmly philosophic, that is, he sought to illuminate the course of recent English political development in order to derive general principles that might, gently and loosely, guide the current navigators of the ship of state. The historian's job, he held, was 'to draw from the occurrences of former times general lessons of moral and political wisdom'. At the same time, as a passionate admirer of Scott, he strove 'to make the past present, to bring the distant near … to call up our ancestors before us with all their peculiarities of language, manners, and garb, to show us over their houses, to seat us at their tables, to rummage their old-fashioned wardrobes, to explain the uses of their ponderous furniture', in sum, 'to reclaim those materials which the novelist has appropriated'.[9] He was also a man who, after his political career was over, was keen to make a steady income off his pen.

This Macaulay achieved triumphantly with his *History Of England* (the first volumes of which appeared in 1848, the last in 1855), regarded even by a jealous rival, J. M. Kemble, as 'a success, I believe, without a parallel in the annals of literature'. In his own day these volumes sold tens of thousands of copies – nearly commensurate with sales of Dickens and Scott – and they kept on selling. Jonathan Rose has pointed out that Macaulay's *History* was one of the few books as likely to appear on working-class as ruling-class reading lists, several generations after its publication. Even the most scathing review by a rare detractor, the Tory journalist J. W. Croker, writing in the *Quarterly Review* in

March 1849, objecting again to the malign influence of Scott, rebounded on its author to Macaulay's credit; the famous gibe was that Croker had attempted murder and achieved suicide.

Croker was indeed too severe. Most of the picturesqueness in Macaulay's text is cleverly concentrated in the famous first chapter, surveying the state of England in 1685. Thereafter, though feats of heroism are recounted, his heroes are mostly high-born, his cadences stately and far from populist, and the story he tells – while national and patriotic – is safely progressive, constitutional and undemocratic: 'epic dignity' is John Burrow's apt encapsulation. It cannot be said that the *History* represents a sell-out to Scott. In any case, Macaulay's was a nearly unique attempt at bridging popular and élite modes of history-writing in the 1850s. Olive Anderson's study of historical reference in popular and parliamentary discourse at this period shows, for example, that parliamentary discussion still revolved around the diplomatic history of the eighteenth century, probing for genteel lessons in diplomatic conduct or falling into self-congratulatory affirmations of progress. History was taught at both Oxford and Cambridge only as part of an essentially political course, paired with either law or political philosophy. At the same time, popular discussion in the public prints was awhirl with 'historical utopias' and fancy dress history in the manner of Scott, 'an affair of the long time span and the bold outline', in which history offered alternative models of identity and a critique of the present.[10]

Macaulay did cut a swathe which others, following in his wake, would deepen and develop. Educated opinion woke to the potential of nationalist history slowly and painfully, but inexorably, as British democracy unfolded in the third quarter of the nineteenth century. A generation of young Oxbridge students who cut their teeth on Mill and Macaulay and experienced a mixed thrill and horror at the spectacle of nationalist revolutions around Europe in 1848, grew up in the 1850s and 1860s to write a nationalist history of their own. In this connection one turns inevitably to Freeman, Stubbs and Green – not, as they sound, a firm of Victorian conveyancers, but rather a subtly variegated trio of late Victorian historians.

Edward Freeman was really the first Englishman to attempt the epic national history that Thierry had pioneered half a century earlier. An active advocate of a widened suffrage, he had no difficulty heroising the English people as a whole and taking their story back to those misty Anglo-Saxon origins which Macaulay would have found vulgar and remote. At the same time, Freeman did not see his history as immediately 'useful' in the ways that Macaulay could claim. National history was inspirational, and meant to gesture broadly at the English people's native propensity for self-government, but it was not a handbook for politicians. This despite the fact that Freeman was himself a committed Gladstonian Liberal who frequently contemplated a parliamentary career and whose most celebrated saying was that 'History is past politics, and politics is present history'. His history-writing simply did not seek to teach specific lessons in the way that apothegm suggests. He was also a conscientious scholar who played a part in the early stages of the professionalisation of academic history, and ultimately cared more about appealing to his fellow scholars than to a wider public. He ended his public life as an academic, in fact, as the Regius Professor of Modern History at Oxford.

Freeman's predecessor in that post had been William Stubbs, later Bishop of Chester. It was under Stubbs that history first became a proper subject of study at Oxford, and it was Stubbs who provided the academic study of English history with its first basic textbooks. Stubbs also began the process of subtly distancing history as a scholarly subject from *all* immediate uses, whether philosophical or populist. In his inaugural lecture of 1867 he offered himself straight away 'not as a philosopher, nor as a politician, but as a worker at history' – the work of history being presented as a good in itself. He disclaimed contemporary applications for that work, insisting famously that 'the past has no power, no moral right, to dispose of the present by a deed in

mortmain'.[11] Still, it was impossible to read his constitutional history outside a Macaulayan framework, telling a
story of gradual development towards greater liberty,
which sanctified present arrangements with the impress of
historical inevitability. The rising prestige of nationalist
history is evident in the very fact that such an austere and
forbidding figure could attain national eminence, the
rough outlines of his history well known to people who had
not read his books and certainly not attended his lectures,
which were notoriously dry.

Of this late Victorian trio, John Richard Green was the
true champion of a popular, national history. Son of an
Oxford tradesman, he was neither Tory nor academic. Like
many young Victorians inspired by history and thwarted by
the lack of a university course in the subject, he became a
clergyman and wrote history in his spare time, through
which he came to the attention of Freeman and Stubbs. His
magnum opus, *A Short History of the English People*, appeared in 1874. It was, and remains, the definitive romantic
nationalist English history, extending Macaulay's time-
frame, his cast of characters and his emotional sympathies
to truly national dimensions, and, crucially, extending
Freeman's and Stubbs's political concerns in social and
cultural directions that had not been properly served since
Scott and Ainsworth. Green acknowledged his debt to
Scott: 'The Gyrth of *Ivanhoe* was an anachronism', he wrote

'Queen Elizabeth Hawking', from the illustrated edition of J. R. Green's
A Short History of the English People (1893)

in 1869, 'but it showed, at any rate, a consciousness that history was incomplete unless it entered into the social life of the people.'[12] Freeman, in contrast, wrote 'too much of wars and witenagemots, and too little of the life, the tendencies, the sentiments of the people'[13] – too little to be popular history and too little to be good history, as well.

The popularity of Green's *Short History* requires some consideration, for it was both very intense at the time of publication and very enduring. Sometimes cited as the last work of history to have claims to be both 'serious' and 'popular' – at least until the current history boom – Green was certainly still being read widely by students in the 1950s and probably later. In its first three editions alone it sold 326,000 copies. Green blended the latest scholarship into a smoothly flowing story with a strong narrative structure that was yet full of character and incident. He was able to do this because he could use as a framework or foundation the story of continuous national political development, set up by Macaulay and lengthened by Freeman and Stubbs, to which he added a much fuller picture of English national identity, going beyond its political manifestations to consider artistic, literary, creative, religious and social expression. He also catered to many different political interpretations by portraying many successive re-makings of English identity, by the Saxons, Normans, Edward I, Chaucer, Elizabeth and Shakespeare, the Puritans, the Enlightenment and the British Empire. There was something for everyone here.

Green's *Short History* appeared at a point when the prominence of history in national life – particularly serious history in book form – was nearing a peak, towards the end of the nineteenth century. Obscure clergymen and musty antiquarians could become public figures by tapping into the pulse of nationalist history. In certain respects this was a key period for the cultural hegemony of 'high culture' in all its manifestations – art, literature and the classics, as well as history – because high culture had begun to reach out and popular culture had not yet gained sufficient confidence or commercial clout to offer 'national' alternatives. So the authority of the great Victorian 'sages' – figures like Mill, Darwin, Carlyle or Ruskin – was strong. Romantic history had the added virtue of seeming to have bubbled up from below. In striking contrast to its twentieth-century reputation, at the time it did not appear to be a tediously didactic imposition. In this it probably benefited from the fact that it had not yet been embraced by schools or universities. History popped in and out of the school curriculum until its status was regularised in 1902; in 1895, primary school children were still twice as likely to encounter needlework as history.

The prestige of history conveyed by nationalism rubbed off on other varieties beyond the realms of Freeman, Stubbs and Green. Philosophic history enjoyed a revival by placing the English national story firmly at the centre of its schemes of universal human development. The English history read most widely outside of England was just such a work of social theory, by a disciple of Mill, H. T. Buckle. Buckle's *History of Civilization in England* (1857–61) is a densely written, densely argued sketch of world civilisation and its progress towards individual freedom, with England playing the role of vanguard and exemplar. His vision was particularly attractive to audiences who felt they were battling slowly but surely towards social, intellectual and political acceptance, for whom Buckle's scientific certainties were a lifeline gratefully grasped. Thus he had a powerful appeal to self-improving English artisans, but also to struggling intellectuals in illiberal states like Russia. Anton Chekhov recalled in 1891 a story that he had read about an over-educated cabby who bored his fares with lectures on Buckle. This appeal – to English artisans if not to Russian cabbies – had been carefully calculated. 'I want my book to get among the mechanics' institutes and the *people*', Buckle wrote to his friend Emily Shirreff in 1858, 'and to tell you the honest truth, I would rather be praised in popular and, as you rightly call them, vulgar papers than in *scholarly* publications ... They are no judges of the *critical* value of what I have done, but they are admirable judges of its *social* consequences among their own class of readers. And these are they whom I am now beginning to touch, and whom I wish to move.'[14] (The Tory Stubbs was put off by this instrumentalism, and presumably by the populism as well. 'I do not believe in the Philosophy of History, and so do not believe in Buckle', he said.)[15]

A different kind of philosophic history was developed in the following generation by J. R. Seeley, who was influenced by Buckle but aimed at a better educated audience including, in the best traditions of philosophic history, budding statesmen. Seeley was Regius Professor of History at Cambridge and an architect of the new history course there. His idea of history was the old philosophic one of the auxiliary to politics; Freeman's adage about politics being present history is more appropriate to Seeley, who used and embroidered upon it. (Green, perhaps not very tactfully, complained to Freeman about this: '[W]hat does he mean by "present" history? 1788 is no more present than 1588, and the Armada tells presently on us as much as the French Revolution ... Moreover, "the end of the study of history is to make a man" not a historian, but "a politician"! What is the end then of the study of politics, or does he consider them one and the same?')[16]

A generation ago, Seeley explained, 'there prevailed a habit of reading history, as we read poetry, only for an exalted kind of pleasure, and this habit led us, whenever we came to a period in which there was nothing glorious or admirable, to shut the book ... I suppose I may say that this way of regarding history is now obsolete. We do not now read it simply for pleasure, but in order that we may discover the laws of political growth and change, and therefore we hardly stop to inquire whether the period before us is glorious or dismal. It is enough if it is instructive and teaches lessons not to be learned from other periods.'[17] In Seeley's writings, notably *The Expansion of England* (1883), history was both instructive *and* glorious. Seeley more than anyone else popularised the view that history had specific lessons to teach, in this case, the lessons learned from the loss of the 'first British Empire' in eighteenth-century America about how to keep the second British Empire in the twentieth century. At the same time, as this particular lesson suggests, he was careful to bend his didacticism to the service of the political nation. He saw his job as not only educating statesmen but also helping them build national cohesion by cultivating patriotism. *The Expansion of England* contributed to the patriotic spirit directly by selling widely – 80,000 copies in the first two years – and, like Green, durably – it was still selling 3,000 copies a year in the 1930s; like Green's, Seeley's book served as an all-purpose textbook until after the Second World War. Thus Seeley made a signal contribution to both of the two main rationales offered for the continuing public importance of history by professional historians in the early twentieth century: the teaching of lessons to statesmen and the binding of the citizenry to their statesmen.

This brief survey hardly exhausts the list of late Victorian historians who were also great public figures – just skimming the surface one would have to add Charles Kingsley, J. A. Froude, W. E. H. Lecky, James Bryce, Mandell Creighton and Lord Acton. These men were novelists, lecturers, politicians and clergy as well as historians. They spoke on all sorts of national issues, not only those that were obviously historical. They were able to do so because history was now seen as central to a proper understanding of the national character and its propagation as a crucial glue for social and political cohesion; and in certain cases because nationalist history had revived the claims of philosophic history to provide guidance for the immediate conduct of the polity. The uses of history were, then, clear; the authority of the 'great historians' to convey them was hardly challenged. But as the nation fragmented and as cultural authority shivered, the centrality and the usefulness of history were called into question.

III

DRIFTING AWAY

1880–1960

If history held an unprecedented, and perhaps irretrievable, high position in national life in the late Victorian period, how did it subsequently lose that position, and why? A conventional place to start would be with the professionalisation of history, as it squirrelled itself away in the universities and lost touch with the general public. That response is conventional because it holds a good deal of truth. And yet it is only a starting point. A more comprehensive treatment must consider the other uses of history that proliferated oblivious to the academy, serviced by others where academics declined to serve; and it must pull out to a still wider focus, locating those diverse uses of history in an early twentieth-century culture characterised by increasing diversity in all fields and pursuits.

About the professionalisation there can be little doubt. Freeman, Stubbs and Seeley were present at its birth. While

Seeley at least felt that history must continue to tutor politicians, Freeman and Stubbs insisted that the study of history made historians, pure and simple. Stubbs's lifetime of devotion to the sources, their compilation and criticism, established a trend towards 'record history', as opposed to the more romantic 'chronicle history' of Freeman and Green. The British were here belatedly following the trend pioneered by the Germans under their tutelary deity Leopold von Ranke. By the late nineteenth century, given the mounting prestige of German science and German universities, professionalisation was seen even in Britain to be the path to the future – although of course the academic dominance of Rankean history in Germany hardly inhibited the parallel flowering there of popular *Volksgeschichte*. As they went about creating history as a 'discipline', professional historians gradually built up in Britain the battlements of their own little world: a professional body, the Royal Historical Society (founded in 1868 on a broader basis but soon boarded and captured by professional scholars); professional journals, first the *Transactions* of the Royal Historical Society (1871), then the *English Historical Review* (1886); and, increasingly, jobs for scholars in universities, although in this period the world of 'scholarship' and the world of 'universities' were not yet coterminous.

Again following Ranke, these early professional historians thought of themselves as 'scientists' – not at all in the sense that they were developing general laws or theories (that had been the goal of the philosophic historians, up to and including Buckle), but in the sense that they were seeking to accumulate data and to refine the tools they applied to the analysis of that data. This curious turn obviously has something to do with the process of professionalisation itself, whereby the practitioners need to make their craft more technical and exclusive simply to justify the gatekeeping, training and career-building machinery they inhabit. But in this case it was also related to a disenchantment with, or simply an exhaustion of, the 'chronicle history' of the preceding generation. 'The long majestic histories are already written, the "great outlines" are already known', wrote the young H. A. L. Fisher in 1894, recommending 'minute and critical study' of history, 'at any rate at the Universities'.[1]

Fisher's version accepted the continuing vitality of the nationalist narrative – or, as it came to be called, the 'Whig interpretation of history', the 'Whig' (i.e., Liberal) notion that the story of English history was the story of ever increasing liberty and prosperity. At the same time, Fisher allocated a new role and a new significance to university historians. Other professionals were less happy with the Whig narrative itself, indicating a wavering of nationalist purpose inside the academy. 'We do not believe nowadays that Britain arose from the waves with Magna Carta in its bosom and that the Englishman was endowed by a special dispensation with a natural thirst for a Parliamentary vote', wrote A. F. Pollard, founder of the University of London's Institute of Historical Research, in 1916.[2] Perhaps a new narrative was needed; but people of Pollard's bent felt it ought properly to await a generation or two (or three) of careful, patient, scholarly, technical research first. Or perhaps there was no narrative at all – no message or moral in history pertinent to the present. The Cambridge historian Herbert Butterfield, in his famous head-on assault upon *The Whig Interpretation of History* (1931), insisted that, far from reading history for clues to present conditions and future conduct, '[t]he chief aim of the historian is the elucidation of the unlikenesses between past and present'.[3] His Oxford colleague Vivian Galbraith went further. 'To live in any period of the past', he wrote in 1938, 'is to be so overwhelmed with the sense of difference as to confess oneself unable to conceive how the present has become what it is.'[4]

What united all these viewpoints was the desire to detach, at least temporarily, the scholarly pursuit of history from the concerns of the present, whether nationalist, philosophical, political, policy or moral. Undoubtedly this turn did a deal of good for the discipline by unhitching it from the grosser utilitarian motives and urging its practitioners on to higher intellectual standards. But it did seem to dictate that history be written mostly for other historians, who could be relied upon to use it properly.

The fact that scholarly historians withdrew into this inward-looking position does not necessarily imply that they were depriving the public of its supply of history. The public would always have alternative sources, if it wanted them, as Scott and his imitators had demonstrated a century earlier. In fact it is currently a subject of hot debate among historians who study early twentieth-century Britain as to whether this period witnessed an expansion or a contraction of the role of history in national life – in large part because it is just at this juncture that 'history' fragments into so many different aspects.

For one thing, if professional historians drew fastidiously away from nationalist history, that narrative had already become so well embedded in the national consciousness that a fleet of less fastidious popularisers was almost bound to enter the market offering their own versions. Would-be purchasers of nationalist history had plenty of tasty morsels to choose from in this period, ranging from those eminent Edwardians Hilaire Belloc and G. K. Chesterton, who from an unusual Catholic position harped happily on the 'Merry England' theme, through the radical–nonconformist (almost pacifist) version promulgated by Arthur Mee, principally to children through journalism and encyclopedias, to the belligerent Toryism of Arthur Bryant that held a special appeal in the 1930s. None of these histories followed to the letter the consensual Whig narrative of the late Victorians; all had an axe to grind, many of them anti-modern axes. Belloc and Chesterton were unhappy about the last several hundred years of English history and harked back to a pre-modern world where the sturdy peasant or yeoman thrived. Bryant was also made miserable by contemporary materialism and hymned the organic community headed by the lord of the manor. There were left-wing versions of the same anti-modernism, such as the work of J. L. and Barbara Hammond, which portrayed the Industrial Revolution as the violent interruption of the Whig narrative and saw in the trade unions, rather than the peasantry or the gentry, the proper antidote to the social ills thus inflicted. These popular histories, therefore, reflected not the blithe confidence of the Victorians' nationalism but a growing insecurity and anxiety about a nation embattled by very un-Whiggish enemies on the Continent, and yet increasingly divided by class and ideology at home.

Popular history had a natural tendency to revert to consensus during the two world wars, however, a tendency evident, extraordinarily enough, in Herbert Butterfield's *The Englishman and His History* (1944) – the very same Herbert Butterfield who had excoriated the Victorian historians for their lack of professionalism and their truckling to popular nationalism. This gap between the 'Two Histories', professional and popular, temporarily united in Butterfield's breast in 1944, was commented upon in a little satirical poem which the historiographer Julia Stapleton recently unearthed from *The Times Literary Supplement* of July 1944:

Two Histories there are in England's isle:
One is of hard sought scientific fact
Got by research laborious and exact
And needing patient teamwork to compile –
A monument that none may dare hold vile,
For thus, it teaches, Truth herself must act,
Whose is the deft and salutary tact
To explode the false, lay bare the forger's guile.

The other pores not over books and deeds,
But lives enshrined in hearts of transient men,
Continuously as age to age succeeds,
And little recks it the revising pen:
It is that Whiggery the nation reads
In its own eyes and every citizen.

And seasons have been when
It has supremely grasped the helm of state,
Making tumultuous passions moderate
And yield to cool debate:

Disarming mobs, gently unthroning Kings,
Forbidding civil war to imp its wings.

Undoubtedly the two world wars marked those seasons when the nation did read its Whiggery, and even sere academics like Butterfield sought to write it. But in the troubled peacetime between the wars, that kind of nationalist history, while still popular, did not play the unifying national role it had played for the Victorians. Rather like religion at the same time, nationalist history had become less central but busier, because more controversial.

Beyond nationalist history, other, newer forms of historical consciousness arose in these early decades of the twentieth century. Every generation in the past century has tended to think of itself as experiencing unprecedentedly rapid social and cultural change; this early twentieth-century generation was perhaps the first fully to realise it and to obsess about it. 'We moderns', they called themselves, proudly but also nervously. One crucial factor was the dawning of the 'information age' with the first application of electronics to the flow and spread of information, boosting its speed from that of the railway to nearly the speed of light, and extending its reach from iron-bound rail systems to a global cable and broadcast network. The media of this information revolution were the now nearly forgotten telegraph (the transatlantic cable dates from 1868) 'wireless telegraphy' (i. e. the radio), from around 1900; and the daily newspaper, which brought all of this instantaneously harvested global news into most people's homes – in 1900, only 1 in 5 or 6 adults read a daily paper, by 1920 it was 1 in 2.

Awareness of rapid change almost inevitably brought with it awareness of a past slipping away. How widespread this latter awareness was, compared to the former, is very hard to assess. Historians are much more conscious now than they used to be of this period as the period *par excellence* of 'the invention of tradition'. As an impetuous modernity wore away 'custom', which had been the normal means by which societies regulated the relationship between continuity and change, 'tradition' had to be invented – either frankly out of whole cloth, or fashioned out of available historical materials – and formalised and ritualised to prevent it being erased in its turn. This process takes a multitude of different forms, not all of which rely very much on 'history'. As Eric Hobsbawm was one of the first to emphasise, for example, across Europe the rulers of the new democracies *c.* 1900 decked themselves in all sorts of invented habits – flags, anthems, uniforms, ceremonials – to help cement the loyalty of the masses, for which purpose historical authenticity was of relatively trivial importance. Here the touch of history was light and transient – already by the 1920s many of these colourful inventions had fallen out of fashion or been discredited.

Some people did respond to the pace of change in the present by clutching fiercely at fragments of tradition as they blew past. This same period is also marked, again all across Europe, by the origins and growth of the 'historic preservation' movement: tradition not so much invented as fossilised. Societies were founded to preserve historical manuscripts, historic buildings, traditional landscapes and townscapes, folk customs, tales and songs. In Britain, the Society for the Protection of Ancient Buildings was founded in 1877, the National Trust for Places of Historic Interest or Natural Beauty in 1894, the Folk Song Society in 1898. On the whole, however, these organisations remained the preserves of small clusters of enthusiasts before the Second World War. More successful were attempts to re-invent traditional rituals for modern settings. Folk songs were taught in primary schools. Modern yeomen plastered Tudor roses and bits of half-timbering on to the fronts of their suburban semis. May Day festivals were revived in villages and small towns, though the most famous and enduring sprang up in the suburban setting of Bromley and Hayes, where a May Queen was crowned annually from 1907 on Hayes Common. From the 1890s many villages staged historical pageants, elaborate fancy-dress parades and playlets involving the whole community. One impresario, Louis Parker, specialised in staging grand spectacular pageants on a professional basis for larger market towns:

Sherborne in 1905, Warwick in 1906, Bury St Edmunds in 1907, Dover in 1908, Colchester and York in 1909.

Some of the same spirit of capturing and savouring vanishing fragments of the past infected inter-war tourism. Buoyed up among the middle classes by the advent of the motorbus and the spread of car ownership, 'exploring England' became a fashionable holiday pursuit, the more backwoodsy and dissimilar to suburban or urban home the better – something more feasible by car than by rail. Inter-war suburbanites were avid readers and users of guidebooks and travelogues purveying nostalgic or mock-nostalgic evocations of 'Ye Olde England', of which the most popular were H. V. Morton's *In Search of England* (1927) and *This Unknown Island* (1932) by S. P. B. Mais, which was based on a radio series. Perhaps to an extent this genre marked a return to the spirit of Scott and Ainsworth, who wrote for a people discovering themselves and their environs. But the spirit of Morton and Mais was subtly different. As their titles suggest, they set themselves up as explorers of a strange rather than a familiar land. They were moved by backwaters and survivals. The adventurer's thrill was palpable; the sense of possession and connection, less so.

How do we assess the significance of all this diffusely historical activity? Historians are unsure whether it represents a defiance of modernity or an adaptation to it, the care and feeding of the past serving as what sociologists call a 'resti-tutive link' to help people manage the pace of change. Pageant-maker Parker was a defiant anti-modernist: 'This modernising spirit, which destroys all loveliness and has no loveliness of its own to put in its place, is the negation of poetry, the negation of romance ... This is just precisely the kind of spirit which a properly organised and properly con-ducted pageant is designed to kill.'[5] How many of his clients, and the larger number of freelance pageant-masters in the small towns and villages, shared this vision? Possibly quite a few, as the pageants and May Day festivals tended to be concentrated in those places which were most threat-ened by modernity – small towns and villages under the cosh from London and Sheffield and Manchester. As with nationalist history, invented traditions were often partisan interventions in a struggle against modernity which 'tradi-tion' seemed unlikely to win. But bits of half-timbering? May Queen pageants on suburban commons? Motor tourism in the Cotswolds? These are harder to see as fiercely or effectively anti-modern.

In fact, nationalist history, historic preservation and in-vented tradition were often defining themselves against (or, alternatively, seeking to temper and accommodate) charac-teristics of the wider modern culture. Many of these histor-ical initiatives, which cluster around the first decade of the twentieth century, were attempts to find and define a solid, unifying core for a culture which seemed to be rapidly losing its coherence. The information revolution had a lot to do with this; contemporary commentators worried about the fragmenting effects of the bitty, gossipy style characteristic of the new mass newspapers. The little cults of history tended to be either vain efforts to stem this flow or, like folk songs, motor tourism and May Queens, got swept up in its flood.

Another revolutionary factor was the commercialisation of popular culture. In the early nineteenth century, popular culture lacked the financial and organisational resources to be anything but local, amateur and fairly casual. Popular nationalism had had no choice but to express itself through the forms and media of élite culture: the novels of Walter Scott or the illustrated magazines provided by improvers and philanthropists. That was already breaking down in the 1850s when popular publishers like George Reynolds, Edward Lloyd and Abel Heywood began to offer what Patricia Anderson has described as 'a generous measure of highly spiced stories and pictures of wronged serving-girls, beautiful and beset heiresses, evil poisoners, corpses, spectres, and chambers of death'.

By the late nineteenth century, as disposable incomes and leisure time grew, and the market became ever more sophisticated, entirely new genres of commercial leisure were made available to the consuming public. Music hall grew from informal entertainments in the back rooms of pubs to splendiferous spectacles in vast purpose-built palaces. By 1892 there were at least 1,300 commercial amusement halls, with seating for 1 million; by 1901 London alone had 320, seating 400,000. The greatest, if not the most refined, was the Alhambra in Leicester Square (where an Odeon cinema now stands) which sat 3,500 in four tiers. Through these halls poured an accelerating stream of diverse turns and acts, as competition hotted up for audiences, and a premium was placed upon novelty and spectacle. Dance, comedy, song, acrobatics and magic were trotted out higgledy-piggledy. At the turn of the century, 142 special trains were laid on every Sunday just to circulate the performers to their next gig. But soon music hall began to be superseded by another new genre, cinema. There were already 4,000 cinemas seating about 400 million customers a year before the First World War, rising to 1 billion a year by the 1930s. Then came recorded music, dance hall and radio.

These were formidable rivals to high-cultural pursuits such as history and art in the early twentieth century. After the First World War, their very novelty weighed even more heavily in their favour. The war disillusioned many people with the totems and talismans of the preceding generation, and they looked consciously to new worlds of science, leisure and consumption to make a break; the old worlds of history,

art and the classics were discredited, along with the sentimental nationalism to which they had been so closely
bound. There was widespread awareness of the decline, for
example, in museum-going in the inter-war years (except to
the Science Museum, which was booming). Historians felt
with some justification that the values of the new mass-
leisure world were to a great extent defined explicitly against
their own. Henry Ford's aphorism 'history is bunk' was
thought to sum up the temperament of the younger generation. 'To the industrial-town child and man the old history of
England has a very slight bearing on his own experience, and
it is not surprising that a certain contempt for the past
should distinguish leaders of advanced urban democratic
opinion', wrote one commentator in 1912.[6] The same sentiments were still prevalent twenty years later. The young,
wrote Eric Walker in 1935, 'are the victims of a mechanical age
and, particularly in the North where the evils of unemploy-
ment are most apparent, they are being forced to seek their
pleasures and relaxations in false mechanical entertainments which are fostered in the towns whose history, if it
ever existed, has been overshadowed by the new chimney
and slag heap'.[7] Worse still was the perversion of history for
the present-minded purposes of the mass media. Alexander
Korda's immensely popular film *The Private Life of Henry
VIII* (1933) was a target of special hatred for its re-fashioning
of historical figures as twentieth-century celebrities.

Charles Laughton as Henry VIII in Korda's film (1933)

On the whole, historians could and did ignore the mass media. A direct challenge to the history that historians cared most about was posed by changes in reading habits. Alongside the new mass circulation newspapers and magazines there developed a burgeoning commercial book market. The number of titles published annually doubled from 5,000 in 1870 to 10,000 in 1910 rising to 15,000 by 1939. Individual titles were selling very many more copies. Though resisted in Britain by booksellers eager to retain respectability and diversity, the concept of the 'bestseller' was borrowed from America. Fiction took an increasing share of the lists of titles and dominated the ranks of bestsellers. Figure 1 charts the growth in the total number of titles published and indicates how fiction's share grew from 8 per cent to 28 per cent of all titles between 1870 and 1939.

Before the First World War the four top selling authors in Britain were all novelists – Marie Corelli, Hall Caine, Charles Garvice and Nat Gould. These names could sell over a million books a year each. Inter-war bestsellers were more diverse, ranging from the traditional kind of light fiction to the new genre categories of detective, adventure, Western and romance stories. Many more books were circulated through public and private subscription libraries, which were at something of a peak in the inter-war years. Reading in general, therefore, did not suffer from the competition of the new mass media. The average household in

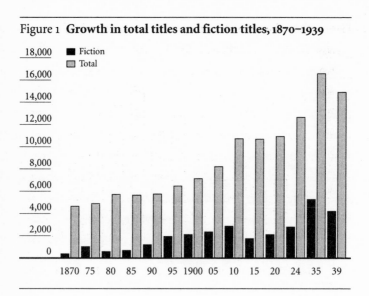

Figure 1 **Growth in total titles and fiction titles, 1870–1939**

1934 spent 2s. a week on reading matter versus 2s. 6d. on entertainments (including cinema, music, dance) and 4s. on tobacco. Cinema probably stimulated reading, then as now, by boosting interest in 'the book of the film'.

Fiction reading at this mass level did not affect history reading much. The one undoubted history bestseller of the period, H. G. Wells's *Outline Of History* (sold in twenty-five parts in 1919), was written on the back of his success as a novelist and author of science fiction. It was by far the best-selling of his books, with an international appeal his tales of English life could never achieve. Similar international successes were later to be registered in Wells's wake

Figure 2 **Number of history titles published, 1870–1939**

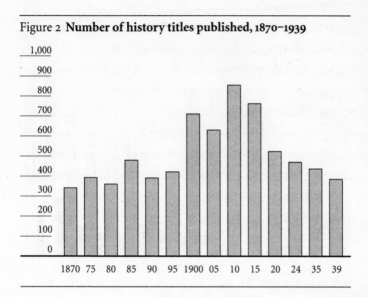

by Arnold Toynbee's *Study of History* (1934–61), and by
Americans Will and Ariel Durant, whose sweeping *Story of
Civilization* (1935–75) was inspired by Buckle. Yet Wells
worried about 'dropping below the novel-reader's horizon
– for good'.[8] The appetite for fiction did threaten to
swamp other kinds of reading, even among the middle-
brow readers who had always been the mainstay of the
history market. The number of titles published is only a
rough indicator of the size of audience, as it makes no dis-
tinction between specialist works, bestsellers and everything in between, but it does tell us something about
publishers' gauge of the market for specific categories.

Figure 2 shows the trend in the number of history titles published annually between 1870 and 1939.

In 1870 there were as many history titles being published as fiction titles – around 350 *per annum*. History titles enjoyed healthy growth until the First World War, though they were being steadily outstripped by fiction – under 900 as opposed to 2,800 fiction titles in 1910. Between the wars, history went into an extended slump. The number of titles fell back to 1870s levels – under 400 a year – in the late 1930s. Its record was poor compared to biography, politics and medicine, indeed compared to practically any other non-fiction category (in what was, after all, a rapidly expanding market), except for essays and *belles lettres*. There was a decided sense that history books were *like* essays and *belles lettres*, elegant but remote throwbacks to the taste of the previous generation.

Contemporaries attributed this decline in the market for history books to the growing appetite for fiction, seeing its debasing effects in the so-called 'biography boom'. The number of biographies published annually between the wars grew rapidly in inverse proportion to the fall in history titles. In the American bestseller lists, biography dominated the non-fiction field: 43 biographies and 96 non-fiction titles in all other categories appeared in the 1929 lists. Had British non-fiction bestseller lists existed then, we might reasonably expect to find a similar pattern. The American experience suggests that the pattern was widespread, and there were mini-booms in France and Germany as well, where Stefan Zweig, André Maurois and Emil Ludwig made their reputations by catering to the biography market. But the English were held to have a special propensity for biography. One survey found that, between 1922 and 1932, 91 political biographies had been published in England, 26 in France, 16 in Germany, 13 in Austria and Russia, 6 in Italy. An old cultural stereotype about the English had it that they were individualistic, eccentric and empirical, and thus had an affinity for the portrait and the biography, rather than history or social thought. Like the Americans, they were thought to nurse puritanical suspicions about the novel which they had formerly sublimated by preferring the more didactic historical novel; as the day of Scott and Ainsworth passed, they were now turning to biography. Of course there was little evidence in the 1920s and 1930s of puritanical horror at the novel. More plausibly, the same forces fuelling the fiction boom were also seen to be at work in the biography boom. Modern consumers wanted something tasty, characterful, above all something they could identify with – written in their own cadences, casting light on their own personalities or providing a plausible idol through which their own thwarted dreams and aspirations could develop. The cinema was tailormade for these functions, providing an endless flow of 'stars' and 'celebrities' for identification and wish-fulfilment. The biography, too, had become cannily more psychological. Here the pioneer was an Englishman, Lytton Strachey, whose *Eminent Victorians* (1918) had triggered the biography boom, by ripping the covers off the three-volume biographical monument that had been standard for the Victorians and substituting in its stead a short, racy, insightful plunge into the depths of his subjects' psyches. 'His bare and metallic art is an epitome of the machine age', pronounced one American commentator;[9] more to the point, Strachey was the non-fictional avatar of the novel age.

Lecturing in 1939 on 'History and the Plain Man', the Earl of Crawford, noble patron of the arts, complained that historians had missed the boat entirely.

> Many of our own historians seem to fear that attention to prose, or rather the effort to make it attractive, must detract from the merit of the history – in short, that history is a picture which requires no frame, a precious stone which needs no setting ... One positive loss is our lack of '*la petite histoire*', which is a notable feature of French literature in newspaper, magazine or plaquette – describing some sidelight or detail or history, thoroughly professional in treatment, and handled with consummate nicety and tact. The composition must have ease and elegance, the prose must be supple and light-handed, with

the discreet measure of imagination; and even if the
subject-matter be dainty, picturesque, or even sentimental, what matters? And all this has slipped through the
fingers of our historians.

Reminiscing fondly about his own youthful enthusiasm for
Scott and Macaulay, Crawford recommended to historians
a revival of their techniques for capturing the popular
imagination.

> Our reading public wants something of the kind. The
> demand is there, and is supplied by the most plausible al-
> ternatives to be found. Authors, publishers, and the com-
> posers of their log-rolling puffs and blurbs, the
> booksellers, too, and the reviewers – all are zealous to cater
> for the buyers of romanced biography or sophisticated
> memoir. This is shallow and ill-informed hack-work,
> badly illustrated and documented – everything, in fact,
> which history should not be. And now historians are
> blaming the publishers, and rating the public for buying
> this poor stuff, which, after all, is evidence of a desire
> which is legitimate and praiseworthy in itself. People best
> qualified to give us '*la petite histoire*' seem to think the
> effort not worth while, or, low be it spoken, that the lesser
> amenities of scholarship are beneath their dignity. It all
> suggests a cleavage between history and art ...[10]

Not all historians were deaf to these arguments. One man above all – beyond the odd wartime effort, like Butterfield's – consistently strove to bridge the 'Two Histories', academic and popular, to repair the cleavage between history and art. He was George Macaulay Trevelyan. Born in 1876, Trevelyan was the grand-nephew of Macaulay and the younger son of a wealthy and artistic Northumberland country gentleman. He had no need to go to work but, his soul having been captured by history, he embarked on the professional academic career that was then just coming into existence. He accepted the first ever Fellowship in History at Trinity College, Cambridge, in 1898 and published in 1899 a learned dissertation on medieval history. Macaulay's shadow hung over him, however, and he could not be content with the cloistered existence of the new professionalised scholar. Throwing up his Fellowship in 1903, Trevelyan embarked instead on a crusade to bring history back fully into the public eye, to revive the great days of the Whig historians. An ardent nationalist, not only for his own country but also for others', he made his reputation as a writer with a great trilogy of books on Garibaldi (1907–11), and then, after war service, a series of brilliant books on British history, culminating in another trilogy on England under Queen Anne (1930–34). In the meantime, he had returned to academia, having accepted in 1927 the Regius Professorship of Modern History at Cambridge. His acade-

G. M. Trevelyan as Chaucer in the Berkhamsted Pageant (1922)

mic responsibilities, which he took seriously, did not inhibit the flow of popular books, by far the most popular of which he published at the height of the Second World War – the *English Social History* of 1944, probably the bestselling history book of the twentieth century (100,000 copies in the first year, over half a million in the first decade).

Trevelyan's amphibious career as a popularising academic was unusual in this period – practically unique. It put him in a special position, able to interpret the one to the other, if only the two histories wished to connect. It also caused him to think more clearly and creatively than anyone else of his generation about the bases upon which history could ground its claim for a place in national life. He first elaborated his views on this subject in a pioneering essay of 1903, 'Clio: A Muse', which stands today as one of the great justifications of history's contribution to the life of the mind.[11] 'Clio: A Muse' was originally written as a riposte to the famous inaugural lecture of J. B. Bury as Regius Professor at Cambridge, 'The Science of History'.[12] Bury's lecture was a paean to the professionalising work of Ranke and his successors. One of its most frequently quoted sections was a passage in praise of 'patient drudgery' and 'microscopic research', virtually for its own sake, without any patent end in mind. '[It] may seem', he granted, 'like the bearing of mortar and bricks to the site of a building which has hardly been begun, of whose plan the labourers know but little.'

This work, the hewing of wood and the drawing of water, has to be done in faith – in the faith that a complete assemblage of the smallest facts of human history will tell in the end. The labour is performed for posterity – for remote posterity; and when, with intelligible scepticism, someone asks the use of the accumulation of statistics, the publication of trivial records, the labour expended on minute criticism, the true answer is: 'That is not so much our business as the business of future generations. We are heaping up material and arranging it, according to the best methods we know ... It is intended for those who follow us rather than for ourselves, and much less for our grandchildren than for generations very remote.' For a long time to come one of the chief services that research can perform is to help to build, firm and solid, some of the countless stairs by which men of distant ages may mount to a height unattainable by us and have a vision of history which we cannot win, standing on our lower slope.

As that closing reference to 'a vision of history' suggests, Bury did have a high estimate of the ultimate use of history. History, 'the handmaid of social science', supplied data for politics and sociology, but more than that, by revealing 'the idea of human development', showed how the whole culture of the present – 'social institutions, law, trade, the industrial and the fine arts, religion, philosophy, folklore, literature' as well as politics – grew out of the past and would grow into the future. But he did not think that the true message of that development would soon be apparent. In the meantime, 'heaping up material and arranging it' was the historian's task, rendered noble by its tiny contribution to this mystical quest, 'the unapparent future ... controlling our perspective'. Bury thought, rather hopefully, that this vision might persuade the taxpayers and private benefactors of the Western world to recognise that 'the advancement of research in history... is not a luxury ... but a pressing need, a matter of inestimable concern to the nation and the world'.

All of this was a red rag to Trevelyan. He knew perfectly well that Bury's programme, while it might in the short term reap rewards by persuading policy-makers that historical research was a 'science' and thereby deserved support, in the long term rang the death knell for history, as it cut itself off progressively from the wider constituency. Sooner or later, the policy-makers would wake up and realise that the 'vision of history' was a chimera, that unlike real sciences history had no practical value. Worse, however, Trevelyan felt Bury was selling history tragically short – missing out its greatest qualities. In 'Clio: A Muse', he defended systematically the position that history consisted not only of the accumulation of facts about the past and the interpretation thereof, but also of the conveying of those facts and interpretations in their full emotional and intellectual value to a wide public – 'In short, the true value of history is not scientific. Its true value is educational. It can educate the minds of men by causing them to reflect on the past.'

Trevelyan proceeded to adumbrate the different sorts of educational value that history could bestow. First of all, history was moral training: by trawling the past for the great variety and depth of human action, it could train the judgement, widen the sympathy, and develop the conscience. The very difficulty of understanding and assessing human action in the past made it more worthwhile. Even biographies could develop these qualities though, because a single biography gave too idiosyncratic a view, the reader was recommended to attempt several at a time. More especially – and here Trevelyan, a good liberal, was hardly immune from contemporary anxieties about the coming democracy – history could 'train the mind of the citizen into a state in which he is capable of taking a just view of political problems'. Then, history could enhance the appreciation of other branches of human endeavour: it refreshed the meaning of great works of literature from the past and heightened the experience of travel. And finally, of course – here the sometime academic was speaking – history *did* also have a scientific function – it sharpened the analytical powers and permitted theories about cause and effect, like the social sciences.

In other writings and doings, Trevelyan roamed further. Unusually for one of his generation, he engaged closely with the newer forms of historical consciousness that had begun to rear their heads around the turn of the century. Not surprisingly, given his landed gentry background, he was particularly enamoured of the old English countryside as an emblem of national identity; more surprisingly, he took advanced views on the people's right to identify with it in concrete ways – to explore it, learn from it, possibly even to own it. Chairman of the Estates Committee of the National Trust, he personally bought land to donate to the Trust to extend public access and in 1941 his brother made the supreme sacrifice of handing over to the Trust the principal family estate and country house at Wallington in Northumberland – then a highly unusual thing for a landowner to do. Undoubtedly Trevelyan had his own nationalist reasons for wanting to cultivate a love of the countryside among the masses – 'without natural beauty', he thought, 'the English people will perish';[13] what was extraordinary for an historian was his willingness to stoop down to the practical level of how people experienced and consumed history in their ordinary lives.

Trevelyan looked back fondly upon the Victorian age, 'the period when history in England reached the height of its popularity and of its influence on the national mind', the period of Scott, Carlyle and Macaulay and late Victorian inheritors like Froude and Green. These men, by accepting that history could be written and read as literature, maximised not only its educational value but also its reach. This heritage his own generation had betrayed. They sneered at Carlyle and Macaulay as too biased and colourful – scandalously readable. 'The public, hearing thus on authority that they had been "exposed" and were "unsound", ceased to read them – or anybody else. Hearing that history was a science, they left it to scientists.' Revising his essay for republication ten years later (in the process carefully excising the stinging rebukes to Bury), he tried to be a little more optimistic. True, 'almost all that is characteristic in the mind of the young generation is derived from novelists and playwrights ... The public has ceased to watch with any interest the appearance of historical works, good or bad.'[14] On the other hand, a new democracy of politics and culture was in the making and historians had a fresh chance to influence it. History as literature was no longer held in such ill repute. History teaching in adult education, secondary schools and universities offered a magnificent field of action. It only remained for academics to rise to the challenge, to write for this new public.

As we have seen, few academics did so, and the climate was hardly propitious anyway. The public continued to drift away and the number of historical works, 'good or bad', fell steadily. What little effort made to rehabilitate the place of history in national life between the wars was devoted to the field of education which Trevelyan had presciently laid out. A Historical Association, principally for schoolteachers but quickly colonised by academics, was founded in 1906. For a time its journal, *History*, engaged in some lively polemics on rationales and methods for the teaching of history in schools. But so low was historians' confidence in the public's taste – or so firm was the grip of the scientific spirit on historians' sense of self – that they fell back on a narrow and disciplinary set of rationales to justify history's place in the curriculum.

History was taught notoriously badly in schools of this period. In public schools, it suffered still from harping shallowly and predictably on the Whig narrative – the mixture of patriotic cant and pat moralising that called forth that wonderful satire on national history, W. C. Sellar and R. J. Yeatman's *1066 and All That* (1930). This sad state of affairs was only partially compensated for by the improved and broadening teaching of history at the universities, where, whatever the limitations of the 'scientific' school of thought, it at least ensured a more systematic approach to evidence and reasoning. In the elementary schools where the vast bulk of the population got its education, history had been made compulsory in 1900, mostly for Victorian nationalist reasons. A torrent of dreary textbooks was subsequently pumped out to cater to it. Patrick Brindle has taken the ingenious view that we cannot judge the quality of history teaching in schools from these textbooks because no one read them, except possibly the teacher, desperately mugging up on the new subject.[15] Mostly, however, history teachers fell back on their own dim memories of Victorian popular history, cribbed from Scott and Ainsworth and Shakespeare, and also grabbed eagerly at new ideas for conveying a difficult subject to recalcitrant schoolchildren: role play, visual aids, outings. Yet there was a widespread view that elementary school children were incapable of the higher forms of reasoning or imagination and that they needed to be drilled with rote learning. In classes of up to fifty, there were practical reasons for this. But it did raise the question, Why bother? What was history in schools *for*?

The standard answer remained the nationalist one. In an oligarchical age, history had been held to be a pleasant and useful part of the training of the legislator, educating the morals and refining the logic of an élite. At the dawn of democracy, when the ordinary citizen was to be the legislator, such moral and philosophical training might be thought equally useful to the masses. In the immediate aftermath of the First World War, when universal male (and even limited female) suffrage was finally granted, historical education could be defended humanistically as a building block of democracy. 'The child must be brought up not only as a gentleman or as a scholar, or an athlete', wrote one commentator in 1918, 'but as the responsible member of a free, self-governing community.'[16]

Unfortunately, the more common version of this argument took on a dark, defensive, controlling tone. The question was no longer, Who are we?, but rather, Who ought you to be? 'England is at present at the mercy of a large electorate, administered by officials, and led by orators whose difficult task is to induce their amateur constituents to condone the necessary work of the experts', wrote Eric

Fulton in 1914 in an essay on 'History and the National Life'.[17] The very first thing that large electorate needed was to be force-fed a national identity, as had happened to the Germans and the Americans. Exactly the arguments that had been made by the great Victorian historians for history as an insight into national character were now repeated more defensively: history no longer revealed the upright character of the nation, it was now a necessary antidote to a debased character. '[T]he influence of the past', wrote H. G. Wood in the *Listener* in 1932, 'is an essential factor in building up character, national and individual ... A nation or race without roots in the past has yet to find itself, has yet to make its contribution to mankind. A nation or race that has lost interest in its past is already on the road to decline.'[18]

Even G. P. Gooch, a close friend and associate of Trevelyan, found himself blending this crude nationalist rationale for history with the higher rationale tendered by Trevelyan – history as ethics and civics – in a 1937 lecture at University College London. Quoting Lord Acton – 'The great achievement of history is to develop and perfect the moral conscience' – he argued that the study of history engendered a feeling for the unity of humankind, developing a tolerance and appreciation of variety and complexity (though he also felt, like Bury, that 'the simple conception of growth from savagery to civilisation' imbued all of this variety with a transcendent meaning). At the same time, history's 'first task' was assuredly 'to enable us to understand the world into which we are born and the stage on which we are called to play our part'.

> The effective training of the British citizen has begun
> when he realises that the greatness of his country rests on
> the related principles of sea power and self-determination.
> The differences between British and Continental mental-
> ity are unintelligible till we recognise that security allowed
> us to outgrow autocracy, to exalt the civilian above the
> soldier, to develop the independence of law, and to foster
> the emergence of the common man. There is no more pre-
> cious element in our national heritage than the sturdy in-
> dividualism which bids defiance alike to subjection and to
> standardisation.[19]

This latter argument points to the other principal rationale summoned up by professional historians on those
occasions when they felt called to do so: the practical application of the lessons of the past to the policy decisions of
the present. In the 1920s, Whig mantras about the unique-
ness and separateness of the English had been seen to have
value as bolsters for national identity, but with relatively
few policy implications. In the 1930s, however, that
changed. The rise of the dictators, collectivism and totali-
tarianism, the questions of appeasement, disarmament,

security national and international – all offered an irre-
sistible temptation for the historian to leap forward with
his lessons. Where Seeley had proposed lessons in imperial
history, Gooch and others tackled diplomacy and international relations, with a soupçon of social policy. Hegel once
said that the only lesson history teaches is that people never
learn from history. The historians set out to prove him
wrong. Gooch, as we have seen, prescribed sea power and
self-determination. H. G. Wood thought the lessons of
history in the same juncture were free trade, government by
consent and national purpose. Eric Walker suggested 'a
spirit of lofty morality and a regard for the fundamental
values of national life as a defence against the facile generalisations of jingoism and bombast'.[20]

'Facile generalisations' surely hits the nail on the head. If
this was the best history could do in the way of lessons, it
was time to give way to social science. After 1945, many historians came to exactly that conclusion.

Nationalist history enjoyed an Indian summer during the
Second World War, if the success of Trevelyan's *English
Social History* is anything to go by. Its social dimension
plucked a chord with the democratic, collectivist mood of
the war and its immediate aftermath. Like all Indian
summers, however, this one was followed quickly by the
chills of autumn. Both nationalism and collectivism went

into a long decline in the 1950s. A society groping towards affluence was finding new satisfactions, new identities, on a more individualised basis. The Americans' re-definition of their own 'way of life', based less on citizenship and association and more now on the acquisition and enjoyment of consumer goods, was powerfully attractive to Europeans, too. The Americans' re-definition of global politics – challenging the old national and imperial loyalties with a bipolar understanding of the world defined by the Cold War – was, if not so attractive, more pressing upon Europeans. Furthermore, to the extent that national cohesion was still on the menu, history seemed like an increasingly implausible recipe for it. That 1930s suspicion that 'history is bunk' festered dangerously in the minds of a younger generation enraptured by plastics, rockets, television and beat music. It was not easy to fit these things into Bury and Gooch's 'idea of development': the present bore little or no relationship to the past.

Suddenly the nationalist rationales for history seemed weak, unpersuasive – and yet they were the only social rationales most people, including most historians, had to hand. If history was inessential for national cohesion, and if national cohesion itself was in question, then wherein lay history's special capacity for training in citizenship? In any case, there were more plausible claimants for that role now, mostly from the social sciences. Surely citizenship was the proper province of politics, social policy of sociology, economic policy of economics. As one honest historian, W. H. Burston, granted in 1948:

> The citizen seeks causes, and moreover, present causes, so that he may deal with present problems. And although present causes sometimes have their origins in the past, they may be changed almost out of recognition by each age and in particular by the present. And in fact the search for historical origins as a guide to sound judgment in current political problems often results in the major fallacy of thinking that when we have explained how something grew up, we have therefore justified its existence as something morally or politically desirable in our present society.

Breaking completely from the long-standing 'official line' on such matters, Burston scorned the idea that debates on reform of the House of Lords, for example, would be well served by lengthy disquisitions on the history of the Upper House over the past 1,000 years.[21] So much for the law of development!

Newer social sciences, particularly psychology, seemed to be more in tune with the younger generation's individualism. One of the intellectual successes of the 1950s was Geoffrey Gorer's *Exploring English Character* (1955), a topic which at any point in the preceding century would have been tackled from an historical point of view, but which in Gorer's treatment was almost wholly psychological. The national characteristics identified by Gorer –

> a great resentment at being overlooked or controlled, a love of freedom; fortitude; a low interest in sexual activity, compared with most of the neighbouring societies; a strong belief in the value of education for the formation of character; consideration and delicacy for the feelings of other people; and a very strong attachment to marriage and the institution of the family

– nearly all could be laid down to schooling and child-rearing habits.[22] So much for history as the maker of character! One by one, the standard rationales for history were being picked off.

Not that the social sciences had it all their own way. They could not cater to the more esoteric and individual types of soul-searching any more than history could. The 1950s were the decade, too, of diffuse spirituality – working its way out of organised religion but not out of a religious framework altogether – of the discovery of Eastern philosophies and of a Western variant, existentialism. When an embittered S. P. B. Mais, wondering after the war why the BBC had dumped him and his historical travelogues, listed his modern adversaries, existentialism was prominent among them, alongside communism, socialism, surrealism, pre-fabs and, indeed, 'progress'.

These trends are reflected in that not wholly reliable index, numbers of titles published. The number of fiction titles was not growing in this period, although this may be due to marketing strategies emphasising a few blockbusters at the expense of diversity; the British were slowly preparing for bestseller lists. The number of non-fiction titles was growing, however. The sciences boomed. Religion, a category which included a lot of spirituality and philosophy, performed particularly strongly. Politics held up; sociology grew from a low base. Interestingly, art and architecture surged ahead, a trend reflected elsewhere in museum attendances – after wartime austerity, colour and stylishness were at a premium. All of these categories moved well ahead of history. The number of history titles published in the 1950s reached its lowest point since records began. From a peak in 1900 representing 10 per cent of all titles, history had shrunk to barely 1 per cent by the late 1950s. Even biography had tapered off.

What was the reaction of academic historians to the history slump? Understandably, they were absorbed by the expansion of higher education, which grew rapidly in the 1950s and accelerated further in the 1960s as the effects of the baby boom kicked in; starting from a very low base,

Britain had a long way to go in this field, compared to most other western European countries. Academic textbooks formed a rising percentage of that small number of volumes published annually. The quality of those textbooks was rising, too, as 'scientific' history reached the height of its prestige and powers. It is notable that many of the textbooks of the 1950s still feel reliable today. Some, such as the works of the Tudor historian G. R. Elton, are still worth reprinting and updating, which cannot be said of pre-war textbooks. Their influence trickled down into the better public and grammar schools. Elton deliberately targeted History A-Level, where 'Tudors and Stuarts' had become the favoured option, not so much for nationalist reasons as because the sources were so well ordered and edited, the political narrative so clear, and, thanks to Elton and his cohorts, the problems and debates so neatly laid out.

This was the 'scientific' history of the university colonising its feeder layer just below, although it hardly represented a hand held out to the wider world, given the still very narrow recruitment into universities in Britain. On those rare occasions when they poked their heads over the parapet, academic historians had little to offer a broader public. Burston, in his frank appraisal in 1948, admitted cheerfully that 'though history may not give us exact parallels to the present, it can give us a valuable, though "second-hand" experience of life'.[23] When the magazine *History*

Today debuted in 1951, its editors were determined to resist too much popularisation in order to retain the respect of academics; they sought, and achieved, a circulation level at about one third that of their French equivalent. Like the Historical Association's *History, History Today* became a place for academics to report the results of their research, speaking to an only slightly extended audience. 'Popular-ized history is mostly dull and valueless', warned Lewis Namier in an early issue, '"popular" history, that which grips and sways the masses, is mostly a figment ... to affect the masses history has to work on their passions and emo-tions, projecting them through a distorted, mythical past into a coveted future.'[24] History in service to the people sounded very Nazi, and it was about to sound very Soviet; history in service to itself was a safer bet.

A few historians *were* concerned by the collapse of the Whig narrative and of Bury and Gooch's 'idea of develop-ment', not for what these collapses portended for their standing in national life but for what they said about history's status as a discipline within the academic world. Little bursts of philosophical contention broke out around R. G. Collingwood's posthumously published *The Idea of History* (1947) and Michael Oakeshott's essays on the phi-losophy of history. A climax was reached with E. H. Carr's 1961 lectures, *What Is History?*, originally delivered in a series honouring G. M. Trevelyan, then broadcast and widely circulated in book form. Trevelyan himself told Carr that after reading Hegel's philosophy of history sixty or seventy years previously he had more or less abandoned the subject. But Carr's book was such a provocation. On the one hand, it eschewed 'science': history was nothing more or less than the historian's interpretation. On the other hand, it embraced the deeply unfashionable idea of progress, in a way returning to the old 'idea of development'. It relativised history by giving the historian's own creative energies freer rein; it objectified history by harnessing it to great modern social and economic transformations. After a short struggle, the profession more or less gave up trying to resolve the paradoxes; it accepted Carr's as *the* book on the philosophy of history, which it remained at least until the 1970s, when I entered the profession. Richard Evans has written that for his generation, the men and women of 1968, the galvanising effect of *What Is History?* lay not in its philosophy but in its politics, making history seem wide-ranging, exciting, and above all relevant. Speaking for my cohort only, I can say that we bought the book dutifully, although we would not have dreamed of reading it.

Such debates over the philosophy of history were given an added *frisson* by the fact that they took place at the height of the Cold War. The independence of the historian was under threat, not only in the Eastern bloc but in the

West, too. Behind the Iron Curtain, the distortion of history for ideological purposes about which Orwell had warned so prophetically in *1984* was sufficiently ominous, but distant. In the West, however, many Continental governments were playing similar tricks with history, especially with the recent history of the Second World War and the Resistance. Each political faction had its own version to peddle. Governments coped with this by assembling historical commissions representing all complexions. This only politicised history further. British historians were rightly proud of their splendid isolation from government. They were a bit frightened both by Carr's relativism – there is no escape in 'science' – and his progressivism, especially as his own academic reputation had been built upon fairly Marxist interpretations of Soviet history.

For most historians, I think it is safe to say, the philosophy of history was felt to be treacherous ground. Far better to justify history's place in the university by affiliating it to the social sciences, which had some claims of their own to be 'objective' and at least seemed in tune with society's aspirations. Carr had given some encouragement to this view, too: 'the more sociological history becomes, and the more historical sociology becomes, the better for both'.[25] Historians began to probe neighbouring disciplines gingerly for problems, techniques and values. Economics and the dawn of the computer age stimulated the development of quantitative methods. Sociology laid out a menu of contemporary problems whose histories could be investigated. Anthropology had the congenial mission of studying 'strange' societies. Of course the Cold War winkled itself into these quarters, too. Each side had its own version of social science. This polarisation gave social science history both its excitement and its predictability. The debates of that period that were still raging when I first encountered them in the 1970s seemed at the time terribly urgent: 'the standard of living question' (did British workers benefit from the Industrial Revolution?); 'the Victorian revolution in government' (did the welfare state originate in humanitarianism or ideology?). In retrospect I can see how much shadow-boxing they involved, in which only the committed could take a real interest.

Unlike the philosophy of history, social science history undoubtedly had a healthy effect on how history was actually practised inside universities. It exposed historians to a range of other disciplines, sharpened up their reasoning powers, forced them to define their problems more carefully and to accumulate evidence more systematically. It supplied new narratives to supplant the old nationalist ones, which were applicable not only to Britain and Europe but to the wider world. Carr drew attention to this in his final lecture, entitled 'The Widening Horizon', tearing a strip off the Cambridge History Faculty for its British parochialism.

But social science did nothing to help historians define what was distinctive about history, less still to broaden their constituency. Carr saw this, too. In notes towards a second edition of *What Is History?*, he wrote,

> History is preoccupied with fundamental processes of change. If you are allergic to these processes, you abandon history and take cover in the social sciences. Today anthropology, sociology, etc., flourish. History is sick. But then our society too is sick.[26]

What was true in the universities was also true in the schools. As history sloughed off its nationalist rationales, it lost its claims to special status and got progressively merged into 'social studies' in the schools which served the bulk of the British people. By the early 1960s, if Carr had asked, not an audience of Cambridge historians but the man or woman in the street, 'What is history?', he might well have received the answer, 'Not much.'

IV

WIDENING HORIZONS
1960 −

From a very low ebb in the late 1950s, popular engagement with history in a variety of old and new forms burgeoned dramatically over the next few decades. Academic history continued its love affair with the social sciences, but at the same time branched out in all sorts of new directions, geographically and thematically; what had been a somewhat closed, proud world was stirred up by the passions of its younger generation. For a long time, however, these two worlds – even though to some extent tossed and turned by the same forces – remained almost unaware of each other's existence. It is only in the last decade that they have begun to intermesh, not to everyone's satisfaction.

The indifference, or outright hostility, to history that had characterised prevailing public attitudes in Britain in the middle decades of the twentieth century gave way in the 1960s to ironic affection, and eventually wholehearted enjoyment. What had perhaps been an excessive reaction against history – 'history is bunk!' – was tempered by a growing appreciation that history was not at odds with modernity, but twinned with it. As Raphael Samuel has suggested, the distintegration of myths of national destiny made it safer and easier for people to forage in the past without feeling constrained or dominated by it. So history began to look less like a burden and more like a funfair. 'Swinging London' developed a penchant for the flea market and the fancy-dress party. The Beatles made witty, modern uses of Victoriana, interweaving their electric guitars with harmonium, steam organ and calliope, and dressing up Sgt Pepper's Lonely Hearts Club Band in mock Edwardian uniforms, as if purchased from the trendy London boutique I Was Lord Kitchener's Valet. All over the country, people who lived in eighteenth- and nineteenth-century building stock stopped trying to hide the fact with chipboard and pebbledash and began instead timidly to strip away and show off the historical fabric that lay beneath. Brick was back. Antiques were chic. Of course this only went so far. No one, apart from a few pop stars, went around in furbelows and farthingales. But history began to be seen as a possible source book for personal expression in a way it had not been for the previous generation.

In much the same way, local and family history and, particularly, genealogy enjoyed a tremendous boom from the

1960s onwards. Some, but not all, of this was about finding one's roots in a changing world (the word 'roots' itself gaining popularity from Alex Haley's 1976 book and the follow-up TV series of that name about a black American's search for his African forebears). In the increasingly mobile post-war world, people often felt that they had no real roots wherever they had ended up; often they were simply curious about other people's roots that underlay the places they now inhabited. Home owners – now a majority of the population – wanted to know about their predecessors. New arrivals wondered about the origins of that deserted warehouse on the corner, or that ornate piece of Victorian ironwork in the park, or the rotting barn in the next field with the curious beamed roof. Here they were reacting, too, against the excessive homogenisation that 'international style' architecture had introduced at its height from the mid-1950s to the mid-1960s, and against the destruction of historic environments in town and country that had gone further in Britain in the 1950s and early 1960s than anywhere else in Europe. Some of the preservationist impulses that had originated in the early twentieth century thus resurfaced, but on a much broader basis, both in the social composition of their following and in the targets of their sympathies. Everything old and unusual was felt to be worth a second look: Victorian gasometers, early industrial machinery, hedgerows, benches and bollards, canals, mills and workhouses. Steam railway preservation was a popular hobby. So was the collecting of 'bygones', a tellingly amorphous category encompassing everything that was 'everyday' and old.

The biggest preservationist success of this period was the National Trust. Before the Second World War the Trust had been viewed as a small, élitist body of philanthropists and enthusiasts. Between the 1940s and the 1960s it collected a magnificent set of aristocratic country houses, whose owners could no longer afford to keep them up, and although this helped build up a new constituency of genteel motor tourists in search of a polite weekend outing it threatened simply to replace one élitist image with another. Cleverly the Trust broke out of this trap in the late 1960s. It made a big push to publicise its long-standing commitment to natural beauty, launching 'Enterprise Neptune' to save the coastline in 1965. It widened the scope of its historic preservation efforts, too, scaling back the prominence of its country houses and scooping up buildings reflecting the wide range of contemporary sympathies – townhouses, poorhouses, lighthouses, even, eventually, a well-preserved inter-war semi complete with original contents down to the packaged foods, and the boyhood home of Paul McCartney. The National Trust professionalised its administration, and particularly its recruitment. In consequence, its membership, which had grown slowly but healthily to 100,000 by 1960, grew to 200,000 by 1970, and then took off – 1 million by 1980, 2 million by 1990. It is today the largest private membership organisation of any kind in Europe.

These historical enthusiasms were represented only fitfully in the mass media in the 1960s. The British, then as now, got most of their cinema from America. The BBC did seek to fill a lacuna with native product on the small screen, and made a hit from the late 1960s onwards with a series of costume dramas, some little more than filmed theatrical stagings of historical narratives (Henry VIII and Elizabeth figured prominently), others full-blown historical re-creations of classic novels or addictive historical serials – for example, the sagas of the Forsytes (1967), the Pallisers (1974) and the Poldarks (1975). Leisure-oriented historical programming started early, with *Going for a Song*, a popular antiques show that debuted in 1965 and made a national figure out of antique dealer Arthur Negus. Negus's follow-up, *Antiques Roadshow*, was launched on an occasional basis in 1977, and as a regular series from 1979, from when it built up huge audiences. There was actually more of this kind of thing than of serious historical exposition. A. J. P. Taylor's lectures to camera, which ran from 1957, were *sui generis*. They had started as a gimmick for commercial television: 'ATV presents an experiment. Can a brilliant historian talking about a fascinating subject hold the attention of a television audience of millions for half an hour?'[1] In

1957 that seemed an unlikely prospect, but Taylor caught the history wave and his lectures became a regular feature of 1960s television. But Taylor had few imitators; not many academics would have been happy – even had they been able – to expose themselves in this way. There was the further problem that credible historical re-creations were expensive. Even the *Civilisation* series, fronted by the art historian Kenneth Clark in 1969, and which drew an audience of 2.5 million, focused very strictly on the art objects at its centre, sketching in historical context only lightly and comparatively cheaply.

This constraint did not, of course, affect programming on recent history for which sound recordings and film footage were available. The 1960s and 1970s also saw the beginnings of the inexorable rise of 'contemporary history', with its special attention given to the heroes and horrors of the Second World War, with which we are still living today. The BBC kicked off in 1964 with its 26-part series on *The Great War*, memorably narrated by Michael Redgrave, and 'collectable' in a pre-video era through the production of a parallel series of glossy magazine part works. Thames Television was inspired to respond with an equivalent Second World War epic. *The World at War* dug up 3 million feet of archive film and 1 million feet of interview and location footage for use in the production of another 26-part series, first aired in 1973–4. These mass media productions of

Kenneth Clark on Iona (1969)

course interacted with family history and genealogy, as war buffs fanned out into the record offices to trace family members' records and decorations, and with historic preservation and tourism, in the form of battlefield sites and tours and war museums. Mass interest in the Holocaust came relatively late, spurred on by the Hollywood film *Schindler's List* (1993) and the fiftieth anniversary memorials in 1994–5. A concrete proposal for a British museum devoted to the Holocaust was not advanced until 1995; it opened as an exhibition at the Imperial War Museum in 2000. In contrast, the United States Holocaust Memorial

Museum had been chartered in 1980. Before the 1990s the Holocaust had been treated in Britain more as an episode in the war, with special attention paid to Belsen, the concentration camp liberated by the British Army in April 1945.

Perhaps most strikingly, the 1960s also witnessed a sudden and dramatic growth of interest in history books, of all kinds. Using our rough index of the numbers of titles published, we can date the turnaround specifically to 1960, in which year the number jumped by a third from 300 to 400. Since then growth in the history book market has continued unabated, apart from a pause in the 1970s, to this day (see figure 3).

History titles now number in the thousands annually. All categories of non-fiction in particular have grown strongly over this period, but history's relative position has improved from 1 per cent to between 3 per cent and 5 per cent of all titles. The most popular of these books do not fit easily into any one category, either. The initial boom of the 1960s built on a revival in traditional, well-crafted English history. Winston Churchill's three-volume *History of the English-Speaking Peoples* (1956–8) and Veronica Wedgwood's three-volume history of the English Civil War (1955–64) may have primed this market. The top seller of 1964 was said to be a gift pack of Trevelyan's *Illustrated Social History*, a grateful nation bidding farewell to its author, who had died two years previously. In the next year

Figure 3 **Growth in number of history titles since 1945**

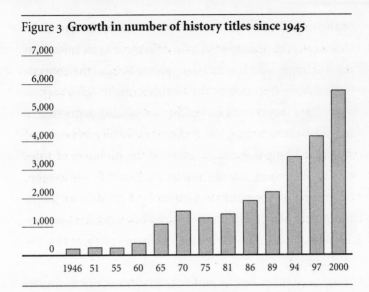

the big hit was A. J. P. Taylor's *English History 1914–1945*, which combined the political and military history of the two world wars with a good dose of people's history in the manner of J. R. Green, but tart, clear-headed and unsentimental, appealing to modern tastes.

However, publishers and booksellers were surprised to discover that modern tastes were suddenly very catholic. Any kind of history could sell if lively, well-written and full of human as well as intellectual interest. The other big seller of 1964 was Steven Runciman's *The Fall of Constantinople, 1453*. Runciman had by then already begun to build up a popular following with a book on another sufficiently remote medieval theme, *The Sicilian Vespers* (1958), which demonstrated, thought the booksellers, 'his gift for reducing the most obscure and complex periods of history to manageable and eminently readable books'.[2] Twenty-five years later Runciman's books were still leading the reprint lists of history publishers. When the history book boom resumed after the 1970s, its ambit widened further. By the 1990s, 40 per cent of titles were published in British history (all periods) and 10 per cent on the Second World War, the other half widely distributed, with surprisingly large concentrations in ancient and African history.

How can we explain this sudden surge in interest in history and what significance should we attach to it? The same difficulties, and the same controversies, that we observed in the early twentieth century attend the historical turn of the later twentieth century. Historians (oddly, you might think) have shown a tendency to suspect popular interest in history, as if it were not quite decent for a modern, forward-looking country. Late twentieth-century historical consciousness is variously described as a fit of anxiety about progress, a symptom of the crisis of capitalism, a marketing trick of the consumer society (thus possibly a symptom of the triumph of capitalism?), a sign of wavering national identity. As we have seen, however, historical consciousness keeps popping up in a variety of forms, bearing a variety of significances, at every phase of modernity. Perhaps it was, rather, the mid-twentieth-century period of aversion from history that was abnormal. And in the case of the current history boom, it is surely impossible to come up with a unifying analysis that explains its success in the 1960s (a decade of social and cultural optimism), the 1970s (a decade of pessimism and national division), the 1980s (a decade of fragmented and divergent moods) *and* the 1990s (a decade of apparent consensus and resurgent optimism).

Whatever the reasons, it is hard to escape the conclusion that, in this period at least, history's profile *was* higher in the wider culture than it had been before. This was possible because, unlike some of its early-century manifestations, it was seen in most instances as unproblematically compatible with modern life. Investigating, memorialising, preserving, enjoying, even wallowing in the past were in fact among the luxuries of modern life, which liberation from the oppressions of the past made possible. Because the nationalist narrative had broken down, people felt more able to tamper with the past on their own – it was now sufficiently remote from the present to give the explorer the desired latitude.

These considerations offer no real explanation of why people chose to explore the past, but only indicate that they were freer to do so than previously. One crucial part of the explanation must simply be distance from the over-eventful history of the 1914–45 period. From the 1920s to the 1950s many people felt that they had lived through too much history to want to accumulate more 'second-hand', and they felt betrayed, too, by the nation-building and lesson-teaching functions of historians, which had proved such dismal failures. By the 1960s a younger generation was growing up, eager to learn about their parents' and grandparents' exciting lives 'second-hand', although a degree of reticence or good manners may have held them back a while.

Then there was the impact of affluence. Rising living standards, burgeoning leisure time and extending physical mobility were widening more people's horizons so that they could participate in the life-enhancing travel and exploration previously available only to a minority. One economist thought to correlate trends in National Trust membership to a cocktail of socio-economic factors, including income growth, reduction in working hours, the extension of education, and the rise of car ownership. The correlation works well except for the 1970s, when Trust membership rose in conditions of socio-economic stagnation: you can attribute this according to your tastes to a wobble in national self-confidence, inducing a fit of nostalgia, or to the professionalisation of the National Trust membership machine. A correlation is, again, not an explanation. It does not say *why* people disburse the fruits of affluence upon coastal rambles and country houses. But they do.

Of those socio-economic factors, the one most pertinent to growth in historical activity – rather than, say, tourism and leisure in general – ought to be education. One of the inhibiting factors we have seen already as limiting popular interest in history was its poor service in most state schools. This had not changed in the 1960s. A 1966 survey of 9,677 boys and girls leaving school at fifteen found that 'history was of small importance and even smaller interest', at the bottom of the table of subjects deemed to be 'useful and interesting' and second from the top of subjects rated 'useless and boring'. The observant Mary Price, who reported these findings to the Historical Association, noted the stark contrast between this and the public's growing fascination for history evident in book sales, film and television, local amenity societies and tourism.[3] But of course the number of people gaining access to much better history teaching at grammar schools, private schools and universities was also growing steadily at this time. For those not leaving school, O-Level and A-Level numbers were keeping up well, although Price noted already a shift of interest away from 'Tudors and Stuarts' towards the nineteenth and twentieth centuries, which would continue over the next few decades. Perhaps the attention devoted by academics to the top tier of the school ladder was paying off, slowly. As their audience there grew, their responsibility would also grow to give that audience some good reasons for continuing the pursuit of history.

But history's appeal demonstrably extended well beyond people at the cutting edge of affluence and rising educational standards. Undoubtedly those doubts about progress and national identity cited earlier played their part: history *could* be a lifeline in a present of uncertainty. Politicians did employ historical arguments to bolster public opinion at junctures where they might otherwise fear a wobble. Thus the 'Dunkirk spirit' and the 'myth of the Blitz' were invoked to portray the English as a tightly knit, self-sufficient community when threatened by 'invaders' (the EEC at various points in the post-war period, the Argentinians during the Falklands War, and in 1990 during the reunification of Germany). Arthur Bryant had used a similar myth of Napoleonic era encirclement when writing at the time of the Blitz. Imperial myths resurfaced at the time of Suez. Margaret Thatcher used 'Victorian values' to dignify her own line of political morality and to damn others. In the 1970s, when the 'break-up of Britain' was predicted, the English told heartening historical stories about themselves for protection against the Scots, and vice versa, just as Bosnians, Serbs and Croats reinvented history to make sense out of the real life break-up of Yugoslavia.

It would be a mistake, however, to generalise from these moments of crisis to explain the length and depth of the history boom. The groundswell of interest in the local, the familial and the particular, for example, cannot be closely connected either to socio-economic trends or to doubts about progress and national identity. Somehow history has become one of the principal theatres within which people explore the possibilities of life, as individuals and as collectives. It is not quite right, I think, to call these 'theatres of memory', as Raphael Samuel entitled his great compendium of insights into contemporary uses of the past, or the work that goes on in them, 'memory work'. 'Memory' implies more continuity than is appropriate; it suggests genetic affiliations across time and generations that need not be there. Of course there are representations of memory like museums, monuments, family histories and collections, but they only capture a single type of historical experience. People also use history more creatively and loosely than that. They often prefer to seek a history that is distant and unexplored. They want to discover, or even create, as well as remember. This is one of the distinctive pleasures of reading history (in the archive, but also on the pages of a book) as opposed to visiting it at a museum or historic site. For the same reason people are not always keen to place themselves in history – to be given a context or a sequence; they might prefer to add the history of others to themselves, to their repertoire of imagined possibilities. Richard Evans has written recently to explain the history boom, 'Old kinds of identity are in decline ... people are turning to history for answers. What we are has to be seen as the end product of a process of becoming, a process that only history can recount and explain.'[4] That may have been a source of history's authority in earlier periods: nationalist history certainly placed people 'as the end product of a process of becoming'. The new appeal of history has more to do with people rejecting their 'place', seeing themselves as artists of their own becoming, and using history imaginatively to assist in that process. We will return to these conundrums at the end, when I want to suggest to which of these historical functions scholarly historians can contribute, and to which they cannot.

Before then, however, we must trace the academics' story from the excitements of the 1960s onwards, to see how or if they responded to the history boom. Historians enjoyed (if that is the word) their own ferment in these years. Grossly over-simplifying, we can identify two major sources of change – social science history and a new kind of people's history.

Social science history was not new in the 1960s, but it wrought its influence in a transformed atmosphere. The gentle thawing of the Cold War and a new spirit of independence amongst the intellectuals loosened the grip of the old ideological orthodoxies. Earlier applications of social science to history had sought to throw backwards in time present-day theories and values, trussing up the past and putting it in thrall to the present. There was still a good deal of that spirit around in the 1960s and 1970s. The great university novel of the 1970s, Malcolm Bradbury's *The History Man* (1975), was not about an historian at all, but a sociologist, who worked his will through wisecracking appeals to historical inevitability. A little bit of Marx, a little bit of Freud, a little bit of social history, went his formula. The historian who latched on to social science was now more likely to use it to show how different the past was – using social science to reveal those differences systematically and in ways that the social science-minded would recognise. 'Since we can only properly understand ourselves and our world, here and now, if we have something to contrast it with, the historians must provide that something', wrote Peter Laslett in 1965 in a classic work of historical demography, *The World We Have Lost*, whose very title made the point.[5] Often the means to this end were anthropological, probing deep into the mentalities of the past to reveal lost or blurred meanings: what the English in the seventeenth century meant by 'magic', for example, in the work of Keith Thomas; or how carnival figured in the lives of sixteenth-century French people, as explored by the American Natalie Zemon Davis. As Davis insisted, the trick to making this kind of investigation a success lay not in exporting present-day anthropological concepts to the past, but rather in treating the past as a 'total cultural system' with its own integrity and letting the fieldwork guide you towards the right concepts. Much of the best of this work appeared in a leading journal, *Past & Present*, which had been founded as a more or less explicitly Marxist organ in 1952 but had been refreshed by an influx of non-Marxist social scientists in 1959.

Social science history generated great excitement within the historical profession. It bid to extend dramatically the range of possible subjects, firmly decentring politics and giving room to all aspects of culture and society no matter how apparently marginal or trivial (sometimes, to probe symbolic value, the more marginal the better). It extended the geographic and chronological imagination of historians, too, giving scholars of the most distant times and places equal status to the modernists who had dominated earlier versions of social science history. Social science history could be said to have 'democratised' history by extending so far its range of subjects. By remaining reliant on social theory abstractions to explore this new subject matter, however, it could not always be said to have 'humanised' it. Riveting new worlds of human experience had been revealed, but the people within them often seemed trapped by structures of thought and social system.

To restore personality and agency to history was the

mission of a new kind of people's history that surfaced at about the same time. Here, unusually, one can cite a single great inspiration – E. P. Thompson's *The Making of the English Working Class* (1963). Thompson had been a leading Marxist historian who had become bitterly disillusioned by the ideological rigidity and political crimes of the Communist Party. He was, by his own account, 'seized' by the spirit of William Morris and his poetic, ethical utopianism. Never very comfortable in an academic environment, Thompson threw himself into adult education in Yorkshire and into political activism, seeking to build a 'New Left' with the rigour of Marxism but without the moral contamination of Stalinism. His greatest contribution to this effort was *The Making*, a book aimed deliberately at a non-academic audience. This wonderful, sprawling account of democratic thought and action in England at the height of the Industrial Revolution worked its magic through a combination of its author's and his subjects' words. The latter Thompson had unearthed from a thousand obscure sources, bringing back to life ordinary people's self-consciousness after generations of burial under what Thompson famously called 'the condescension of posterity'. Thompson's own words made them into a great work of history, an unrepeatable combination of bristling polemic, vivid, startling re-creation, slashing historiographical argument – and, yes, a bit of social theory, too. Thompson defended his approach in a special issue of *The Times Literary Supplement* in April 1966 on 'New Ways in History', under the heading, 'History From Below', and the movement he inspired has travelled under that name (or, alternatively, 'the new social history') since.

'History from below' was more explicitly political than most social science history. It put itself at the service of politically disenfranchised groups who had also, as history had grown up embedded within a political structure, been historically disenfranchised. It was therefore closely connected to the student movement (for whom Thompson became one of the few older generation role models), the women's movement (a women's history 'from below' had taken off by the early 1970s), and later ethnic and sexual minority rights campaigns. This may have limited its appeal to the wider world – it is hard to think of another book deriving from this camp that had anything like the same audience as *The Making*, including Thompson's own later books – but it may have deepened its impact on the university, as these movements became staging grounds for Ph.D. programmes in the 1970s, and many of its leaders kept their political commitments going by taking on part-time teaching and adult education jobs.

In addition to making history seem more 'exciting' and 'relevant' to the younger generation, these two currents also engendered a new self-consciousness about history's place in society among both their enthusiasts and their adversaries.

In the late 1960s and early 1970s all parties took opportunities to put forward their views on the purposes of history. New claims were staked, and 'scientific' historians, who had long stifled such questions out of a desire to distance themselves from romantic nationalism, were forced to define their *raison d'être*. The social scientists were, perhaps, the least likely to think in this way, for to them the method was itself the message. They were busy enough revitalising the discipline with new sources, subjects, techniques and theoretical perspectives not to need to worry, yet, about what a revitalised discipline was for. If social science history had a mission, it was the same as social science's, that is, to derive prescriptions for policy-makers. 'History from below', on the other hand, embodied not only new subjects but a new sense of purpose. Writing 'history from below' was a creative act and a political duty, a gesture of respect to the undeservedly neglected and forgotten which signalled a revival of the causes and values they had stood for. Though they would never have put it that way, these new social historians were using the past to stimulate their moral imagination in just the way Trevelyan had prescribed as one of the most powerful functions of the discipline.

These claims for relevance and inspiration called forth from G. R. Elton that last great statement of the scientific view, *The Practice of History* (1967). Geoffrey Elton, originally Gottfried Ehrenberg, had come to Britain as a Jewish refugee in the 1930s, trained as a Tudor historian with Sir John Neale in London, and by the 1960s had become a leading figure in early modern British history at Cambridge. He was the epitome of the highly professionalised historian who saw history as a 'specialised form of inquiry', autonomous of other disciplines, and in that sense – the sense that had come to dominate academic history in the mid-twentieth century – 'scientific'. The immediate stimulus for *The Practice of History* was provided by that April 1966 issue of the *TLS*, especially a contribution by Keith Thomas called 'The Tools and the Job' that aroused Elton's ire by seeming to treat history not as a 'science' on its own but merely as an auxiliary to the social sciences. Although the nub of Elton's creed was that the historian ought to 'study history for its own sake', and most of his book was devoted to questions of method and professional training, Elton did try, in an extended opening chapter on 'purpose', to re-state the mission of scientific history. The new methods, he said, were either not new or not historical; that is, they projected back on to the past inappropriate frameworks in a spurious quest for novelty or relevance. As for gleaning inspiration from the past, that was the aim of the amateur, not the professional historian. It was just about possible to get a glimmering of sympathy with the past from amateur study; it was all too easy to get sentimental. 'That really fine amateur historian, G. M. Trevelyan, achieved both.' (This, for those unaccustomed to Eltonian irony, is a deep cut.) Most troubling of all to Elton was the renewed attempt to find an inner logic in history, as Carr had done, and as the Marxists were doing. This was endangering the freedom and autonomy of the academic that for Elton were the most valuable qualities of the British university. The progress of the discipline could only be assured if it followed its own road, not Moscow's or Washington's or Rome's, or even Mr E. H. Carr's.

After these serial acts of demolition, Elton left himself only a few paragraphs to offer his own answer to the question, Why should we study history? He granted that the study of history was generally found to be 'agreeable' – 'many people simply want to know about the past' – and that it may have some remote practical value. It is a little disappointing to find even Elton falling back on that cliché, 'Historical knowledge gives solidity to the understanding of the present and may suggest guiding lines for the future.' But ultimately he stood up for its autonomy: 'the study of history is legitimate in itself, and any use of it for another purpose is secondary'.[6] It is a training of the mind, but it only trains the mind by staying honest to its own terms. And given that Elton also defined 'its own terms' rather narrowly – it was not permissible, for instance, to mingle historical evidence (which mostly lay in written records) with other kinds of evidence (archaeological, literary or anthropological, for example) – the intellectual gain achieved by studying history was unlikely to spill over into non-historical pursuits. Elton was rather sceptical that history might have any general educational function. His chief concern, as his closing chapters confirmed, was the making of more professional historians, the university-centred view of history's mission that had arisen in the early years of the century.

Other historians were, however, prepared to make the wider educational claims for history that Elton eschewed. Medievalists, in particular, were inclined at this juncture to be reflective about the purposes of history. They had never been able to appeal as modernists had to the popular idea of history as teaching lessons – revealing inner logics or pointing out recent mistakes – and the nationalist claims, which professionals had long foresworn but which quietly underpinned popular interest in medieval history all the same, had by now almost entirely melted away. They were therefore frankly willing to admit that the emperor had no clothes, and then to begin, gingerly, to re-dress him. In a 1969 radio broadcast, for example, Gordon Leff addressed directly the 'lessons of history': surely no one believed any longer that history taught lessons either in a direct or even in a philosophical sense? 'Even when we invoke history's verdict it is meant more as a figure of speech than as a conviction that history will really judge.'

No doubt, in certain situations, parallels with the past can provide a moral boost, as with the parallels drawn in 1940 between Britain's situation then and in 1800. But most of history does not revolve around such comparisons, and when it does the result is usually history at its most jejune ... history, although it is directed to the past, is essentially about the new. It is read and written as the unfolding of events which by definition have not occurred before. That is the only reason for their having a history. If Hitler's invasion threat in 1940 had been identical with Napoleon's in 1800, no separate study of Hitler's would be needed: we should merely say, 'For Hitler in 1940 see Napoleon 1800.'

Leff was braver about saying what history could not do than about staking new claims. He did, however, refer back to Trevelyan's suggestions about the unique opportunities offered by studying people's actions and choices in a past unfettered by the concerns of the present.[7]

Another medievalist, Sir Richard Southern, in his inaugural lecture as Chichele Professor at Oxford in 1961, had shocked Elton by daring to speculate on how the decline of nationalism and imperialism might affect the university market for history. In his Rede Lecture of 1977, he propounded a relaxed, expansive, optimistic idea of the uses of history, without lapses into utilitarianism, of a kind that

had not often been heard previously from the lips of professionals.

> We must not expect too much of history. It will not tell us
> what to believe or how to act; it will not make us more tol-
> erant or more ecumenical or more peaceful. But if we are
> any of these things – or even *per impossibile* if we are the
> opposite of these things – it will add a new pleasure and
> breadth to our understanding of what it is we are. History,
> emphatically, is not everything; but it is an aspect of every-
> thing ... As a necessary aspect of every subject it will con-
> tinue to grow, and as it grows it will add a new pleasure to
> every subject.[8]

Southern's balancing act between modesty and ambition
points to the dilemma facing historians making claims for
their discipline at a time when social science was so pressing. On the one hand, it was necessary to refuse the analo-
gies between history and social science that might lead
people to expect from history the same kind of immediately
useful 'lessons'. On the other hand, there *were* educational
values history had to offer which the social sciences could
not. The Regius Professor at Oxford, H. R. Trevor-Roper,
made similar points in an article in *Past & Present* in 1969, a
nudge aimed at his more sociological contemporaries. 'We
must not expect too much from the study of history', he

urged, but it can broaden our horizons, enlarge our views and deepen our judgement.[9] When the prestige of social science is broken, he did not quite say, history's time will come again.

Trevor-Roper was not a medievalist. He was a Renaissance specialist, but he was well known for his wide-ranging interests, including the most contemporary. His most famous book was probably his youthful reconstruction, initially at the behest of British Intelligence, of *The Last Days of Hitler* (1947), and, notoriously, he met his historical downfall in 1983 by lending his name to the credibility of the spurious 'Hitler Diaries'. It was a healthy sign that the people who had the most to gain by promoting the utilitarian claims of studying recent history in particular were willing to forego them. From this point of view, the most important statement of all was that made by the military historian Michael Howard in 1981 when he succeeded Trevor-Roper as Regius Professor at Oxford. In his inaugural lecture, 'The Lessons of History', he began by repeating his predecessor's view that history, like other humanities, could not rely on 'professional' rationales but needed to reach out to the lay audience. He flirted with the long-conventional argument that history was a useful training for citizenship, that '[t]o know the way in which our society came to be formed, to have some understanding of the conflicting forces that created it and are still at work within it, is not only an advantage in the conduct and understanding of affairs: it is indispensable'. But then he backtracked suddenly from so instrumental a view. In fact, he said, the understanding conveyed by history is too broad and too general to compare with the understandings offered by the social sciences. 'It is safer to assume that history, whatever its value in educating the judgement, teaches no "lessons" ... The past is infinitely various, an inexhaustible storehouse of incidents from which we can prove anything or its contrary.' The man on the street might find this maddening.

> He looks for wise teachers who will use their knowledge of the past to explain the present and guide him as to the future. He finds workmen, busily engaged in tearing up what he had always regarded as a perfectly decent highway; doing their best to discourage him from proceeding along it at all; and warning him, if he does, that the surface is temporary, that they cannot guarantee its reliability, that they have no idea when it will be completed, and that he proceeds at his own risk.

But it would be foolish for historians to pretend otherwise. He then proceeded to make a number of more constructive arguments, some newer than others. There were the horizon-broadening functions alluded to by Trevelyan: 'If we are properly to educate the laity ... [w]e have to teach them how to step outside their own cultural skins and enter into the minds of others.' In an even stronger echo of Trevelyan, Howard claimed for history 'a training of the judgement and of the imagination', which could not be achieved simply by 're-creating our own past' – though he then rather spoiled his flourish by calling for special consideration of the Americans' experience, as 'a society which more than any other is likely to shape our lives'. More innovatively, he warned against the pitfalls of state and media-nourished historical myths. 'Our primary professional responsibility', he insisted, 'is to keep clear and untainted those springs of knowledge that ultimately feed the great public reservoirs of popular histories and school textbooks and that are now piped to every household in the country through the television screens.'[10] However negatively, here at last was a suggestion from a leading academic practitioner that there *was* another history out there to which academics might have something to contribute.

For what is curious about most of these statements of history's purpose is how closely oriented they were to developments inside the profession – the impact of the social sciences, 'history from below' – and how little connection they bore to the growth of a historical consciousness in the wider world. There were a number of reasons for this disconnection. Ignorance was one. Historians had now spent many generations inside universities, progressively insulating themselves with the disciplines of 'scientific' history from their bad old nationalist origins. They were dimly aware of the publishing boom – commented upon, at least, by Eric Hobsbawm in the *TLS* symposium, and, mordantly, by Elton in *The Practice of History* ('The whole business is beginning to show the marks of a runaway boom: hectic production leading to dilution of quality').[11] But the parts that interested them most were the textbook markets, aimed at their own students rather than outsiders. Even 'history from below' read mostly as if it were written for fellow graduate students, or, at best, fellow activists; it was not 'people's history' in any easily recognisable sense of that term.

Another factor was the healthy insistence on autonomy, the suspicion of calls from political movements and government for history to be put to some 'higher' service – which had had such disastrous consequences elsewhere in Europe. But there was a less healthy snobbery that lay behind that suspicion (a whiff of which can be caught in Howard's fastidious references to tainted waters). A. J. P. Taylor was never forgiven by many colleagues for airing his views in the popular press and on television. When the scientific historian Lewis Namier was asked to advise on the appointment of a new Regius Professor at Oxford in 1957, he vetoed Taylor

on precisely these grounds. Trevor-Roper was appointed
instead. To Trevor-Roper's credit, his own view had been that
'the Regius Chair should not go simply to specialists in ten
years of history but to someone who can interest people in
historical problems regardless of such cramped frontiers', by
which he meant someone like Runciman or Taylor. But if the
powers-that-be were to reject both Runciman and Taylor,
'then who am I to spurn this unexpected crown?'[12]

Suspicion of television in 1957 may have been a widespread fault; but it lingered among academics, and among
historians more than most. As late as 1987, the Oxford historian John Roberts felt he had to make professional
excuses for the time he had devoted to a thirteen-part BBC
television series on world history. He worried about the
pace of television, the tendency to edit, compress and sim-
plify, the false atmosphere of resolution which its neatly
scripted films gave, and the temptations to 'recreate' historical situations for which no authentic visual images existed.
But in the right hands, he concluded – meaning the right
historian twinned with the right producer – the benefits of
mass appeal could outweigh these drawbacks. '[T]elevision
can go where literate high culture has failed to penetrate',
and might be used in order to establish 'a core of national
history which would be part of our common culture'. And
for the future, 'we may hope for growing sophistication and
knowledge among even a mass audience'.[13]

Academic suspicion about the historical sensibility of the wider world only darkened in the 1980s, as the political atmosphere changed. It was often observed about Margaret Thatcher's election victories that, unusually for a Conservative, she did better among the less well-educated portions of the middle class than among those with university degrees. There was certainly a strong mutual enmity between the Thatcherites and the academic profession, not helped by the fact that Thatcherism fell in the middle of a longer period of declining academic salaries and growing bureaucratic interference in university life. Historians were among the most vocal critics, partly because of their own leftward shift in the 1960s and 1970s, partly because their subject did particularly badly in the retrenchments of the 1980s. This period saw the establishment of a History at the Universities Defence Group and a Campaign for Public Sector History to defend the shrinking position of history at all levels of higher education. Historians also resented bitterly Thatcher's revival of the nationalist uses of history that they thought had been long buried. In fact, some rather good history was written as direct ripostes to Thatcher's historical homilies. Angus Calder began his book on *The Myth of the Blitz* (published in 1991) out of anger 'over the sentimentalisation of 1940 by Labour apologists, then over the abuse of "Churchillism" by Mrs Thatcher during the Falklands War'.[14] More petulantly

Anthony Barnett wrote a whole book, *Iron Britannia* (1982), in the immediate aftermath of the Falklands War, decrying the same conflation of Churchillism and Thatcherism. A segment on the BBC's historical news magazine programme *Timewatch* – my own little contribution – criticised Thatcher's invocation of 'Victorian values' in the 1983 General Election campaign. Nicely 'balanced' with contributions from New Left historian Raphael Samuel and New Right historian Maurice Cowling, the central argument – that Thatcher's Victorian values were a Frankenstein monster of bits and pieces scavenged out of context for political purposes – was itself a blatantly political intervention, though *prima facie* a spectacularly unsuccessful one.

Hostility to the Thatcherite uses of history deepened academic suspicions of popular history, further postponing the day when the two worlds would again find points of overlap and common interest. Hostility and suspicion certainly hovered over the so-called 'heritage debate' of the 1980s. The opening salvo was fired by the academic-turned-journalist Patrick Wright, who published in 1985 a difficult book called *On Living in an Old Country* which quickly gathered a considerable audience, in academic circles at least. Building on the social theory of Agnes Heller, Wright was one of the first to propose that historical consciousness flowed naturally out of the everyday conditions of modernity, as people used historical particularities to 'make sense' of and possibly to

're-enchant' ordinary lives tossed about in a rapidly changing world. He then subjected to close analysis a series of
points and moments at which this historical consciousness
had been exploited (although not entirely aggrandised) by
the political right. This, he suggested, was something more
substantial – and more dangerous – than Thatcher's evoca-
tion of Churchill to rally the nation behind the Falklands
campaign; it was sinking its teeth deep into the nation's guts.

A few years later some of Wright's themes were picked
up and elaborated on in more polemical form by the critic
and historian Robert Hewison, who had been writing a
series of books about British culture since the Second
World War. Having got to the present, he was horrified to
discover 'a climate of decline', a culture leached of its potential for creativity and optimism. The chief culprit was 'the
heritage industry': the accumulation of conservation
bodies, museums, government agencies and voluntary societies that had been building up since the early part of the
century, but especially since the 1960s, devoted not to creating culture but to fossilising it. Hewison defended the function of a proportionate historical consciousness in helping
people adjust to social change – 'Without knowing where
we have been, it is difficult to know where we are going' –
but he felt that the historical consciousness of his own day
had tipped over into nostalgia, weighting too heavily the
pull of the past and obscuring the way forward.[15]

The 'heritage debate' was not much of a debate, at least inside the universities, where Wright and Hewison found few dissentients. The idea that historical consciousness was a sign of the morbid decay of English national identity and, worse, of a Tory plot to prop that national identity back up, was pretty much 'hegemonic' (to use a favoured word of the day) in historians' circles by the late 1980s. The last straw was the Thatcher government's plan to install a national school curriculum, mooted in the mid-1980s and legislated in the Education Reform Act of 1988. Thatcher's ideological mentor, Sir Keith Joseph, had announced in 1984, when Secretary of State for Education, in a speech to the Historical Association, his personal preference for a compulsory history curriculum up to age sixteen, with a special emphasis on national history. His successor Kenneth Baker was a well-known sentimentalist about the national history, who was to publish in 1988 an anthology of English history in verse. Both men raised hackles by drawing heavily on the old Whig narratives in recommending a national history which told a story of ever-growing liberty and democracy. Perhaps the historians had been right all along to bunker down in the universities, if the only viable basis for popular history was a refurbished nationalism and a culture saturated in conservative longing for the lost glories of Nelson and Churchill?

In fact, historians' worst fears were not to be realised. The national curriculum debate turned out to be just that, a real debate, with outcomes creditable and satisfying to all sides. In retrospect it also appears to have coincided, at least, with the beginning of a rapprochement between academic and popular histories, which continued to develop and deepen over the ensuing decade.

As the observant pointed out at the time, from the outset Keith Joseph's tone had been conciliatory. While commending the study of national history, he had said emphatically that 'national' did not mean 'nationalist' or even 'patriotic' history. In fact he argued strongly for the need to study British history in an international context, the modern period in the *longue durée* (Joseph was among those troubled by the growing fascination with the horrors of the twentieth century), and even his treasured English 'liberty' in tandem with other value systems. One of his most forceful points was that history had the unique ability to transport us into the mindsets of people very different from us – something rather close to the 'empathy' which was supposed to be the province of the trendy teacher in pursuit of 'relevance'. If there was a utilitarian thread to Joseph's argument, it was his view that history was 'useful' not for building national character but for developing economically productive skills – use of English, numeracy, the assessment of evidence, descriptive, analytical and critical skills. In a separate historical debate, Joseph had been accused of inveighing against the *excesses* of historical consciousness in Britain, as gumming up the works of the Thatcherite 'enterprise culture'. His position on the uses of history in a modern society was probably not all that different from the common-sense position of most working historians.

To their credit, historians woke up to the opportunity. A lively debate was conducted in the historical periodical press, in the pages of *History Today* and *Past & Present.* Among the most passionate and constructive of the controversialists was Raphael Samuel, a champion of 'history from below' who had been rather sympathetic to the Hewison critique of Thatcherised history. But Samuel had been coming round recently to the democratic potential of history, poking his nose into those vast and spreading fields of history-making very far from the academy: the family and local historians, the antique and old photo collectors, the house restorers and flea market frequenters, the historical re-enactors and the steam railway preservers. (He would later document his travels in these circles in *Theatres of Memory.*) All of a sudden his impatience with the closed shop of the academic world burst out. Why should historians be so down on history? Was not the introduction of the national curriculum an unparalleled opportunity to save history in the schools from inevitable extinction in the swamp of 'social studies'? If a stalwart of the academic left like Samuel could see this, there was hope yet for a meeting of minds.

The curriculum that resulted was drafted by a working group of diverse composition, including two academics, Alice Prochaska and Peter Marshall. It managed to preserve the best of the new methods of teaching history that had trickled down from university practice, such as the 'patch' and 'topic' approaches, which encouraged the development of critical, analytical and empathetic skills. At the same time, it tried to restore the sweep and vision of history that tended to get lost in these vertical plunges into historical time, by exposing children to the full range of British and world history, organised chronologically. The only real disadvantage to this mode of organisation was that 14-year-olds would finish off the national curriculum at the 'end' of history, i.e. the twentieth century, and this further reinforced the trend towards studying only modern history at post-14 levels. Surely, however, this trend has more to do with the mass media exposure of twentieth-century history than with the organisation of the curriculum. Surveys of the curriculum in practice found the medieval portions (at age 11–14) among the most popular, and the range of favourite topics spread widely from the Second World War to the Wars of the Roses, from Martin Luther King to Napoleon. Nor did the curriculum seem to have cultivated an uncritical view of the national history – equal numbers reported items that made them proud to be British (the Industrial Revolution, the Second World War) and those that gave them grounds for shame or reflection (slavery, cholera, the First World War). Most importantly, history was now firmly implanted in the primary school curriculum where it had once been threatened with extinction.

In a triumphant essay in the *London Review of Books* in 1990, Raphael Samuel hailed 'the return of history' as 'one of the more remarkable pedagogic reversals of our time'. 'Social studies' had been successfully disaggregated and the special qualities of historical study preserved. More provocatively, he credited 'the restoration of history to the school syllabus and the present vitality of the subject' at least in part to 'the commodification of the past as a source of pleasure and enjoyment … its popularity as a hobby, a holiday pursuit and a form of mass entertainment'.[16] School history had connected with the identity-building, experimental, even utopian impulses that lay within the recent boom in popular historical consciousness.

Another Thatcherite initiative, equally unexpected to most historians, brought that popular historical consciousness on to the doorsteps of the universities. After a decade of remorseless retrenchment and bureaucratic harassment, a decision was taken around 1990 – again, largely for modernising purposes – to boost Britain's very low levels of participation in higher education up to something approaching average European levels. This was to be achieved by merging the 'lower tier' (polytechnics, colleges of higher education) and the 'higher tier' (universities) into a single university sector, and expanding student numbers at all levels. Although the 'unit of resource' (the amount invested per student) dropped steadily until the late 1990s, when it levelled off, the number of students rose much more quickly and absolute levels of funding were up markedly year on year. The scale of this change was dramatic: student numbers doubled between the mid-1980s and the late 1990s, and by the end of the decade participation rates in higher education edged towards 40 per cent. From being the province of a very small minority, the university had suddenly been propelled into the age of mass culture.

History was possibly not best positioned to benefit from this overnight transformation. The new university clientele had been conditioned for generations to think of their futures vocationally and these expectations were bound to transfer, at least in the short term, into quasi-vocational preferences at A-Level and university. History, as we have seen, had stood studiously aloof from vocationalism, or indeed from any self-presentation that might smack of salesmanship. Historians were still only just trying out their newly discovered humanistic rationales. The revitalising effects of the new school curriculum would take some time to work their way through. However, the mere fact that history had won a place in the compulsory curriculum to age 14 – which on the trends of the 1960s and 1970s it might well have lost – kept it in the running. History teachers in schools geared up to try to attract the new mass cohort at 14–16 (GCSE) and 16–18 (A-Level). Understandably, they emphasised some short-term utilitarian values; for example, that history was (among other disciplines) a good training in the evidentiary, analytical and expressive skills that employers valued. They also grabbed at some of the more lurid features of mass media history to 'sell' history to cautious 14- and 16-year-olds and their parents. This borrowing from mass media presentations added further impetus to the trend towards studying only twentieth-century history (and principally its more unpleasant bits) – what some critics have called sourly the 'Nazification' of history – though it is possible to exaggerate that trend. My own study of one examining board at A-Level in 1998 suggested that 30 per cent of candidates were taking principally twentieth-century options while 20 per cent were still studying topics principally pre-1600. The longer-term effects are as yet hard to discern. Not until 2004 will the first cohort of students have passed all the way through the national curriculum. Meanwhile, the numbers of GCSE and A-Level candidates in History have remained fairly stable throughout.

It is also much too early to tell how this will play out for history at the universities. In the early 1990s, when numbers of everything were rising in higher education, the numbers of history departments (at new universities) and history lecturers (at all universities) grew rapidly. There was something of the speculative bubble about this activity, and some of those infant departments are now closing down or shrinking. Undoubtedly the base remains much broader than it was in the 1960s, as a much higher proportion of pupils studying history at 14–18 years carry that study over to higher education. Whatever the long-term effects, in the short term academic historians have had to become much more alert to the diverse ways in which the mass market encounters history outside the university. They often start out their history courses now by asking students about the differences between the presentation of history in the media and in the university. And they offer hybrids – courses in 'heritage', for example, both as a topic in history (the rise of popular historical consciousness in the twentieth century) and as a variant historical practice (how museums present history). However one feels about this – and in the concluding chapter I will consider both pluses and minuses – it has without doubt had the salutary effect of sharpening up historians' ideas about what *is* distinctive about their own practice, what it shares with and where it differs from those other forms of historical consciousness, now no longer hidden in the realms of darkness.

The expansion of higher education has certainly had

something to do with that manifestation of popular historical consciousness which has had the greatest relevance and interest for academic historians, the rise of the 'popular yet serious' history book in the 1990s. As we have seen, the numbers of history books published, and probably total sales, had been mounting steadily since the 1960s, part of the rising tide of histories of all kinds. What was new in the 1990s was that a more academic type of history book began to nudge its way into the mass market. As early as 1989, Simon Schama's *Citizens*, a dense, roiling panorama of the French Revolution by a leading academic, had been a bestseller in both the US and the UK. Linda Colley's *Britons*, a highly analytical study of national identity in eighteenth-century Britain, surprised a lot of booksellers in 1992. A real breakthrough came in 1994, with the publication of Stella Tillyard's collective biography of a set of eighteenth-century noblewomen, *Aristocrats*, which got on to the bestseller lists in both hardcover and, unusually, paperback.

By this stage publishers were waking up. The cinematic one-word titles (often masking considerable sophistication inside) testify to the influence of the marketeers. Fiction had stalled, so non-fiction represented a potential growth area, and history and biography were, to everyone's surprise, among the leading non-fiction categories. They began by reissuing a lot of their backlist in new, quality paperback series. Old biographies of Ataturk and Kipling were dusted off and jostled with histories of the Maya and Ancient Rome and the evergreen Runciman and Taylor. Publishers were rather puzzled at first by the demand for such books. When I surveyed the editors of these quality paperback series for *The Times* in 1993, I registered a lot of embarrassment mingled with surprise: 'there's nothing *élite* about these books at all'; 'they're not *medicine*'; 'I *hate* the word academic'. They had not done any market research and could not even make a stab at guessing why quality history books were selling well. When I suggested that the expansion of higher education might have something to do with it, they looked blank: What expansion? Echoing the previous decade's automatic responses, they all assumed that the university market was being cut back 'savagely'.

Taking their cue from the market, however, publishers began not only to reprint but to commission books on the *Citizens* or *Aristocrats* model. Biography had, of course, been a long-standing non-fiction seller; 'what is more surprising', wrote the trade magazine the *Bookseller*, 'is the extent to which the celebrity scoop has been overtaken by biographies of serious historical figures'.[17] After *Aristocrats*, the next big thing in this category was Amanda Foreman's biography of *Georgiana, Duchess of Devonshire*, the eighteenth-century Princess Di, another paperback bestseller. But not all these 'serious historical figures' were eighteenth-century aristocrats: beneficiaries of the 1990s biography boom ranged from Karl Marx to Henry VIII, Eleanor of Aquitaine to Galileo's daughters. Dava Sobel's *Longitude* (1997) started a trend for biographies of utterly unknown figures with historically important stories: in this case, the clockmaker John Harrison and his race to win a prize for the first accurate measurement of longitude. There followed the stories of a madman who was one of the principal contributors to the *Oxford English Dictionary*, the chemist who invented the colour mauve (paving the way for the full range of modern artificial dyes), the sea captain who controlled the nutmeg trade and laid the foundation for British North America, among others. These biographies took on many of the features of the novel, just at the moment when many novels were taking on historical subjects – indeed, the genre is known in the trade as 'narrative non-fiction'. The same could be said of the non-biographical history books hitting the bestseller lists at the same time, full of vivid characters, Dickensian panoramas, a lot of swashbuckling word play and careful plotting: Antony Beevor's massive hit, *Stalingrad* (1998), in an always popular tradition of military history, but also Orlando Figes's sprawling canvas of the Russian Revolution, *A People's Tragedy* (1996) and Roy Porter's *London: A Social History* (1994), which deftly spans the centuries from the Romans to the present.

The bestsellers were only the tip of the iceberg. Beneath

them was a dramatically extended market for serious
history books of all kinds, at more modest but still by past
standards very high sales levels. They were of all types:
vastly ambitious surveys of the whole of British, European
and world history; little miniatures of narrative and analysis, catching great movements on a tiny pivot; the Second
World War, of course, but also the first millennium, Aztecs,
the Renaissance and the newly fascinating eighteenth
century. What is interesting about this panoply is not only
that publishers were willing to publish them and readers to
buy them, but also that academic authors were willing –
and able – to write them. A new generation of academic
authors had grown up that was not afraid of a more
popular market, nor constrained by academic *politesse*
from writing their hearts out. Nor were they concerned so
much about their independence; perhaps to some extent
they were, ironically, 'Thatcher's children', fed up with poor
public sector salaries and conditions and attracted by the
substantial advances now on offer. Having jealously
guarded their independence from the State in the immediate post-war decades, and thus built up the diversity of their
profession, they were now preparing to enjoy that independence in the marketplace.

A number of the pioneers had been students in the
1960s who had been caught up neither by social science nor
by 'history from below', but somehow breathed in instead

the general excitement about history manifest in the wider culture. Among them were many students of one man, the Cambridge historian J. H. Plumb, who had steered his protégés purposefully away from the severities of Elton: Simon Schama, Roy Porter, John Brewer, Linda Colley, David Cannadine, Norman Stone and Niall Ferguson, to name a selection. It took a little time for this generation to blossom; most published conventional specialised monographs in the 1980s, but unbent in the more promising publishing environment of the 1990s. Younger academics coming from behind them grew up in this new environment: one can now find examples of first books, even on fairly technical subjects, that are being written, pitched and published with a much wider market in mind.

Academic adventurousness has extended beyond the world of books to the mass media. Simon Schama's first dip into television, a series to accompany a book, *Landscape And Memory* (1995), was not a success – too talky and low budget to work as television. Other experiments built confidence. Ian Kershaw served as academic impresario of a methodologically innovative BBC series on the Nazis, impressing with its substance as well as its visual impact, despite the lowering subtitle 'a lesson from history'. The BBC, which in the mid-1990s had revived the sequence of costume dramas launched in the late 1960s with dramatisations of George Eliot, Austen and Dickens, added historical docudramas to

Simon Schama in front of Kenilworth Castle (2000)

the mix; for example, a big budget television version of *Aris-tocrats* in 1999. Historical re-enactments, in which ordinary people sentenced themselves to live weeks and months in a '1900 House', a '1940s House' and an 'Edwardian Country House', were effectively intercut with specialists explaining how these re-enactments differed from the historical situations on which they were based. At the end of the decade Simon Schama and David Starkey had become full-blown television personalities with popular series on British history. Historical programmes could get audiences of 3–4 million – about four times the size of A. J. P. Taylor's 1958 television audience. There had been a time when Taylor was the only 'telly don'. Now there were dozens of them.

By the end of the century, then, the divide that had opened up since the beginning of the century between the worlds of popular and academic history had begun to close. Separate spheres remain, but between them now lies a thick stretch of overlap and intermingling. Historians are battling it out with novelists and scientists for the public's attention, that increasing share of the public who are represented now in the universities, and the larger and attentive public who browse in the bookshops or sit in front of their televisions. That is where the historians will have to be, if they wish to preserve history's traditional place in the university curriculum, defend its new-found place in the school curriculum, and extend its reach in the popular consciousness outside of education.

It is easy to celebrate this re-engagement of historians with the public as a return to the glory days of the great Victorians, of Macaulay and Freeman and Green. But those glory days were built on a popular appetite for history as a recipe for national identity – a rationale few historians (and probably not many more of the public) would care to rely upon now. The 'scientific' historians moved away from it for good reasons. Nationalism put a straitjacket on the way history was practised, and after the First World War the association between history and nationalism began in any case to lose its popular appeal. Thereafter professional historians took refuge in their professional bunkers. This protected them from the worst kinds of 'people's history' promoted by totalitarian states, and in liberal Britain, where the universities remained relatively independent of the State, it protected them from the weaker forms of politicisation prevalent in the Cold War West. In this sheltered environment, the practice of history did gradually diversify, opening up to a bewildering host of new subjects and methods, potentially of interest to a much wider audience. But academic history remained very inward-looking; even ostensibly democratising currents, like 'history from below', were terribly scholastic in tone and temperament.

As history rediscovers its public, then, it will have to redefine its purposes, without losing the scholarly integrity it has built up over the last century. Beyond nationalism, history does have other intellectual and imaginative functions in a modern society. It is *not* just another form of 'infotainment', interchangeable with fiction, and the scholars writing popular history are doing something a good deal more constructive than 'dumbing down' a once respectable discipline.

So what does history have to offer now?

V

THE USES OF HISTORY

The uses of history are still as G. M. Trevelyan tallied them almost one hundred years ago, but they now have relevance to many more people. And there are many more worlds of history now, too, than Trevelyan – relatively acute about such things – dreamed of. The tricky questions arise where those new worlds of popular historical consciousness touch upon, or collide with, the traditional preserves of the academic.

First and foremost, history remains an intellectual discipline as the scientific historians had always insisted. It is, as Elton said, 'an activity of the reasoning mind', though surely not exclusively so. In common with the social sciences, history ought to develop the capacity to identify problems, to accumulate relevant evidence, and to assess that evidence: to measure, to judge, to balance, to compare. Being history, it has special claims to being able to assess change over time, to separate and determine causes and effects, and to identify and compensate for scarcity of data. For these purposes it can borrow theories and structures from those social sciences based in the study of the present, and it can lend its own distinctive data and situations to the construction of new theories and structures. Being history, with its incredible breadth of subject matter ranging over thousands of years of human time, it also lays special burdens upon the memory; most of its data are not machine-readable and they must be mastered, juggled and ordered by the naked human mind. Sometimes lay people say they have no talent for history because they have no 'memory for dates' – but, really, dates are the least of it. The integrated, multifactorial history that is rightly insisted upon nowadays tasks the mind to keep in play a bewildering host of dates, facts, actors, levels of causation, spheres of human activity and shades of meaning in order to produce the best resolutions.

Even scientific historians who kept their heads down in the mid-twentieth century, insisting that each period had an integrity of its own though the temptation to derive 'lessons' from history was so great, often succumbed to the conviction that the processes they studied in the past could at some level of abstraction be linked to the present. This same temptation operates today, especially among the larger proportion of historians whose province is recent or even 'contemporary' history. Not many historians pretend any longer that history teaches direct 'lessons', in the sense of repeated scenarios which can be re-played the second time for the better, but many continue to fall back on orotundities such as 'you can't know where you are or where you're going without knowing where you've come from'. Flattering though this is to the *amour propre* of the historian, it ought in honesty to be avoided by all but the most contemporary of historians. Of course those who study the recent past are in as good a position to offer predictions and prescriptions as those who study the present. But you do not have to go very far back in time to lose this capacity almost entirely. Historians of the eighteenth century, a vogue period just now, have a fatal tendency to drew pretty pictures of 'modernity' as it was being born in their period, and then to draw a straight line from these origins to the present – in the process nearly always doing violence not only to the present, but also to all the intervening periods. Even if the historian can tell a continuous story from some distant origins to the present, the *historical* bias is likely to over-weight the elements of continuity and give a distorted picture of the present. Which is not to say that elements of continuity ought to have no weight – only that historians are not always the best people to judge how much weight to give them, relative to novelties of which they may be less well aware.

Scientific history also took for granted that these 'higher' intellectual functions were only accessible to a few. For most of the twentieth century history was held to be beyond the reach not simply of all primary and most secondary school students, but also of the 98 per cent of the adult population that ended their education at school. Today, the national curriculum assumes that some of these functions are accessible to 11-year-olds, and all of them to the half of the adult population that will attempt a university degree. The democratisation of intellect further saps away at the historian's oracular or lesson-teaching functions, though it builds up an educational function.

While the scientific historians emphasised the intellectual capabilities of history, Trevelyan sought to give greater weight to its imaginative capabilities. Simply put, the study of history broadens the mind. It exposes the student to the full range of human possibilities, only a small sampling of which is available in the present. If the social sciences feel with justice that historians ought not to over-burden the study of the present with the legacies of the past, then historians can respond with equal justice that the limited range of present-day values and behaviours ought not to constrain the contemporary imagination of what is possible for the future. This feeling is if anything reinforced by modern trends towards global homogenisation. As Christopher Harvie, a historian of modern Scotland, once asked plaintively, 'Was it all to be jeans, trainers, t-shirts, baseball caps, in-line skating, fast food?'[1] History reminds us that it was not always like that. At its most ambitious, it so immerses us in alien environments that it allows us to 'empathise'. At its best, it can cause us to 'empathise' *and* to understand, intellectually, at the same time.

The imaginative capability of history is closely connected to its ethical capability. One of the purposes of historical time travel is to transport our modern selves into alien situations which allow us to highlight by contrast our own values and assumptions. Sometimes it is easier to examine complex ethical questions honestly and openly in an historical than in a contemporary setting, the distancing involved taking out some of the heat of the moment without disengaging entirely contemporary values and attitudes. In this aspect history asks us not to lose ourselves in the past but to view the past from our own standpoint; in fact, one of its functions is to help us define our standpoint more clearly. Nowadays we call this 'the search for identity'. The collective identities that people once inherited and had to live with, whether they liked it or not, have broken down: 'community', religion, social hierarchy and class, ideology, nation. Identity is now a much more individualised business, which means both that people have to construct it for themselves and also that they are freer to tailor it after their own fashion. The very idea that people have or need an 'identity' is, however, a contemporary construction. This 'identity' is not so very different from what used to be called philosophy or morality, and similarly the 'identity-building' function of history is not so very different from what the ancients called 'philosophy teaching by example', or what Trevelyan and his contemporaries thought of as exercising the moral imagination.

Fiction rather than history used to be the preferred vehicle for this activity, if only because historians had been puritanically shy of probing the moral and psychological dimensions of their subjects, whereas from the eighteenth-century origins of the novel those dimensions had been the unerring target of the fiction writer. As history took on social and cultural perspectives from the social sciences, and developed its powers of empathy through 'history from below', it began to shed its inhibitions. Today history may have advantages over fiction in its ability to claim that the moral and psychological situations it depicts are 'real', although the continued necessity to mingle the strangeness of the past with the familiarity of the human raises hurdles with which fiction can dispense.

The identity-building functions of history pose a challenge to the historian. The modern reader may not be seeking wider horizons so much as an affirmation. If we travel into the past keeping our own standpoint intact, we may be tempted to find too much of ourselves there. This was the

challenge that historians advising the 1900 House and its successors had to face: if the situations offered were too strange,
participants and viewers could not 'relate' to them; con-
versely, if the participants and viewers were invited to 'relate'
to the situations, then they might easily mistake their own reactions for those of the people who had actually lived them.
The corset today seems a bizarre, pointless and oppressive
device: if you put one on, you are likely to be more struck by
its abnormality than by how it was experienced by those for
whom it was normal. In these circumstances the historian's
job is to be the past's advocate, constantly jabbing the
modern observer in the side with the strangeness and difference of the past, to offset the effects of phony familiarisation.

Because people often have very individual goals in exploring the past, historians cannot always be helpful to
them. Your interest in the history of your own house, or your
local park, or your grandfather's military service, or your
great-grandparents' census records, is about *your* sense of
place in time and space. It might be enhanced by, but it does
not require a broader understanding of, other people's histories – the history of urban development, or military or
social history. The fact that these distinct enterprises often
draw on the same sets of records has been a mounting source
of annoyance to scholarly historians for the past few generations, as the local historians and genealogists crowd into the
record offices and bring the websites crashing down.

But local and family history has built up a political constituency supporting the record offices that ought to be re-
spected. The national repository of government records,
the Public Record Office at Kew, has managed to extract
substantial sums of money from government because it
serves so well a mass constituency of citizens tracing their
ancestors, and in the process has immeasurably improved
the service they give to the records themselves and to the
scholars who also depend upon them. The same principle
ought to apply to the national heritage of print stored in
public libraries. One probably apocryphal story has it that
the British Library could have digitised its entire out-of-
copyright collection for less money than it cost to build its
new home at St. Pancras. Making the national heritage of
print freely available on the web would revolutionise both
popular and scholarly history simultaneously. In any case,
the gap between the family and local historians and the
scholarly historian is not nearly so wide as it once was, if
only because the ordinary citizen's children are far more
likely now than previously to encounter the scholarly world
at university. A-Level History offers an 'individual study'
option, where students choose their own research topic,
and the most popular recourse is to adopt a local or family
history topic that can be researched at a nearby library or
record office – a choice that then flows smoothly into academic history on a university course.

If historians have a slightly vexed relationship with the lay reader's quest for individual identity, then the quest for collective identities – especially national identity – is most problematic of all. As I have argued throughout this book, the mass audience for history arose from an effort to define a collective identity, the nation, whose warrant lay in the past. Professional historians were among the early beneficiaries of this process, and even the scientific historians, who thought they were disentangling themselves from it, rarely did. At least through the 1930s, and in certain respects right up to the 1960s, professional historians thought the one surviving public justification for history was its value for citizenship: teaching lessons in decision-making and giving the new democracy a sense of common purpose. But over the course of the twentieth century, historians soured on this rationale, asserting their independence from the State *and* the public. They often had good reasons to do so, seeing how prostituted historians were, grievously in the Soviet bloc, but in Western Europe and in America, too, where national identity remained a shibboleth which historians were often asked ritually to salute. The climax of this distancing process in Britain was reached in the heritage debate, when most professional historians declared 'heritage' to be bogus and quite distinct from 'history'.

Now that the threat of the State has receded somewhat, and the grassroots character of much of the recent history boom has become clearer, we may be in a better position to judge just how separate heritage and history are, and what contributions historians can and cannot make to the heritage industry. First of all, national identity simply is not as potent a force as it once was in Britain. Those who argue that we are experiencing a 'crisis' of national identity like to hint that this crisis means a strengthening rather than a weakening; the evidence is to the contrary. Much is made of the fact that an increasing number of people now think of themselves as 'English, not British'. But the increase starts from a low base – from 7 per cent in 1997 to 17 per cent in 2000 – though the figures are, and have always been, higher for those describing themselves as 'Scottish, not British' (32 per cent in 2000). Neither measure tells us anything about how much national identity of any kind weighs against other identities. Most surveys which ask people to weight national identity against other sources of identity – family roles, the local community, individual values and attitudes – have found that national identity is of dubious and decreasing personal significance to all age and social groups in England.

So it may be that the heritage industry is not seeking (or at least not able) to shore up national identity at all; it may be rather more about leisure and entertainment, and, where history comes into it, about education, as well. This was a phenomenon of which Trevelyan was already aware a hundred years ago, when he recommended the study of history as an enhancement to the literary and touristic activities of a gentlemanly élite. Many of the leisure activities that were traditionally the preserve of an educated minority have since expanded to cater to an educated majority – visits to art galleries and museums, the reading of non-fiction and literary classics, and visits to heritage sites, too. The mixture of entertainment and educational values in the heritage industry poses some of the same questions for historians, as have been raised above in our discussion of identity-building. Historians continue to worry, rightly, about marketing imperatives in the heritage industry that seem to require 'easy access' to the past, making it as familiar and inviting as possible in order to maximise the audience. To the extent that the heritage industry does still subserve a national identity, it will also want to present an edited and sanitised history that highlights whatever qualities and episodes people currently associate with their nation and its history. Here again the historians' role is to be the advocate of the past, defamiliarising where necessary without having to be discouraging: if people did not have some appetite for the difficulty of the past, they would find their entertainment (as they would find their identities) in more comfortable and convenient materials. The heritage industry knows this, which is why it often wants and needs historians' *imprimatur* in order to verify the 'authenticity' of the historical experience on offer. National Trust and English Heritage guidebooks nowadays often carry footnotes and bibliographies freighted with academic sources. As the professionalisation of the heritage industry gathers speed, the authors of those guides themselves are more and more likely to be people with postgraduate degrees in history, an increasingly common qualification for the work of interpreting history in landscape, architecture and material culture to the general public.

More problematic is the historians' proper relationship to 'tradition' and 'memory'. Appeals to tradition for its own sake manifest themselves now comparatively rarely in Britain – traditions that still live do not require appeals to support them, and 'traditions' that are fading cannot be propped up in this way. The way in which both the law and the constitution function reflects this reality: they rest on 'precedent', but they change by decree whenever precedent is found wanting. The Burkean idea that 'tradition' acts as a necessary and effective brake on change dates from a period when change was suspected or feared more than it is today. In fact it could more accurately be said of modern British history that tradition has helped to pave the way for change, in the same way that we have seen history functioning as a restitutive link between past and future. Tradition does sometimes continue to work in this way today, as, for example, at those periodic outbursts of royal ritual – most recently, a wedding (Charles and Diana) and three funerals (Diana, Margaret, the Queen Mother). Whose job is it to orchestrate and comment on these rituals if not historians? Yet historians know all too well how recently these 'traditions' have been invented, that their content is contemporary rather than historical. Historians' expertise is thus either irrelevant or deflationary. This is why we have those odd categories of 'constitutional expert' or 'authority on royal protocol', people who are happy to invent traditions for public purposes (more often politicians than historians). In these circumstances, historians have the difficult choice of playing killjoy (pointing out how novel these rituals are) or shutting up (understanding the public's need for a bit of make-believe). Happily, such circumstances do not arise very frequently. After the death of the Queen Mother, we will probably have to wait until the next coronation until historians are again tempted to join in this re-invention of tradition.

Most difficult of all is the historian's encounter with popular 'memory', and in particular the current fascination with the horrors of the Second World War. Much of this fascination stems from the peculiar situation of the present generation, impressed by their parents' and grandparents' experience and by the contrast with the comparative un-eventfulness of the present, at least in the West. My own father, a refugee from the Nazis whose life brushed up against both fascism and communism, entitled his memoirs *Interesting Times*, implicitly suggesting to my generation, what many of us believe, that our own times are not nearly so interesting. How should historians respond to this unusual fixation? As with the wider contexts for local and family history, historians can provide tough intellectual contexts for material people are initially drawn to for its personal and/or dramatic content. There are certainly as intellectually respectable problems and questions raised by the two world wars and by the Holocaust as by earlier epochal events in world history. Some of the most influential history books of the current wave, by the likes of Eric Hobsbawm, Joanna Bourke, Mark Mazower or Richard Overy, have been efforts to contextualise the most attention-grabbing events of the twentieth century in just this way. They are important entry points to serious historical treatments of other, more remote situations. As objects of popular 'memory', the prominence of the mid-twentieth-century events will eventually fade, as the events of the First World War are already fading. The memorials and museums devoted to the Second World War and the Holocaust will become background, often unnoticed, just as the myriad First World War memorials have become part of the landscape. For the communities most dramatically affected and retaining a strong collective identity, like the Jews, these memories will get incorporated into that identity – as the delivery out of Egypt had been thousands of years previously incorporated into Jewish ritual and through ritual into identity, or as the experience of slavery is being today ritualised into African-American identity. Otherwise, the injunction 'never forget' will be regarded principally by historians. They will not forget, because it is their job not to forget not because it is part of their 'identity', or because it will teach a 'lesson'.

It is possible, therefore, to continue to distinguish a discrete role for historians even as they come up against or get drawn into quests for individual and collective identities that preoccupy lay people for their own reasons. The same principle applies to history in the mass media. It is not always appreciated how much scholarly history lies behind the presentation of history on radio and television. A very large number of academic historians are all too aware of this, as their phones nowadays ring off the hook with calls from radio and television researchers seeking to air their hunches or to get some free leads. Often they come with their own agenda and it is a battle to shift or change it. This struggle was perhaps inevitable in the days when academics were loath to engage with popular history; thus if they offered supplicants from the media anything, it came in a form rendered deliberately, high-mindedly indigestible. In those circumstances, researchers had no choice but to devise their own agenda and hope for the best that they might be able to wrestle the academic contribution into something useful. Minds are more open on both sides now. Journalists and historians are not after just the same things, but they are better prepared to recognise those differences, accommodate them, and build on points of common purpose. In one of my own recent experiences of collaboration on a television series, I found that the producers had a strong narrative line in mind at the outset but that by the end of the collaboration this had opened up into the kind of flexible, multi-stranded, non-deterministic story which academics prefer to tell – and which can, in capable hands, make for a more exciting (and not necessarily more confusing) visual experience. Thanks to technological advances, it is also possible to interleave scholarly and popular presentations of history in the mass media, cutting back and forth between computer-simulated scenarios or re-enactments and expert commentary to indicate what the grounds for the simulation might be and what lies in the realm of pure speculation. This technique has been used effectively in popular archaeology programmes and spectacularly in a Channel 4 television series on the Neanderthals; it is only a matter of time before it is applied to full-blown historical re-creations.

Writing twenty years ago, Michael Howard suggested to his fellow academics that their relationship to popular history was 'our primary professional responsibility': 'to keep clear and untainted those springs of knowledge that ultimately feed the great public reservoirs of popular histo-ries'. Put that way, it was an arm's length function. Now his-torians carry the waters of knowledge all the way from the springs to the reservoirs, watching closely every step of the way. They do this on the whole not to substitute for the im-presarios of popular histories, but to complement them. There is no need for that collaboration to blur the roles so that historians start behaving just like marketeers and en-tertainers, and there is a good deal to be gained by having a hand in every stage of the process. There is intrinsic value in keeping the springs of knowledge 'clear and untainted', but there is greater value in ensuring that the supply also reaches the consumer in something resembling its original state.

As journalism becomes more frenetic and competitive – and non-fiction radio and television *is* the mainstream of journalism today – the role of the scholar becomes if any-thing more important to the journalists themselves. They know perfectly well how little time they have for research and how much they rely nowadays on sources like the in-ternet or other journalists, with few or no quality controls. This applies to all fields but history is peculiarly vulnerable, because historical myth, once it enters circulation, cannot be checked automatically against people's personal experi-ences or other data just lying about in the present.

More historical myths are put into circulation in this

casual way by journalistic insufficiency than by deliberate and malign manipulation by the State and other sources of authority. For example, one reads often that the experience of old age today is a novel one because 'in the past' life expectancy was very short; few people lived beyond thirty or forty years. This happens not to be true. 'Life expectancy' is an average; it was lower in the past chiefly because child mortality was much higher; for the majority who lived beyond infancy, old age was a common experience. This particular factoid probably does not do much harm. A falling birth rate and medical advances are, in fact, changing the age distribution of our population, which creates a real problem to be discussed. The factoid is a convenience for journalists who want to attract readers' attention to this real problem and are tempted to over-dramatise it by making it appear more novel than it is. Probably the contemporary prestige of history adds to the attraction of providing even a spurious historical dimension to an issue of the day. On the other hand, journalists do not like to make mistakes any more than ordinary mortals – probably less so, because they get corrected in public – and if properly informed would be perfectly well able to do without this mistake. Correcting the mistake itself has benefits: it presents an object lesson in reasoning; it may cause journalists and their readers to reflect in a different way on the contemporary meaning of old age.

To take a more trivial but probably more typical example: I was writing recently about the rise of the 'creative industries' in post-war Britain, and came across a journalistic factoid to the effect that 'about 70 per cent of Japanese computer games are designed within a 30-mile radius of Liverpool'. This factoid seems to have originated in an even more inflated formulation – 70 per cent of the *world's* computer games – in a 1997 report by the think tank Demos. From there it flowed (with gathering authority) into publications of the Foreign Office, the British Council, and the Royal Academy of Engineering, picking up the Japanese dimension somewhere along the line. In that form it was repeated several times in the *Guardian*, once even described, in a June 2000 piece on the hi-tech economy in Liverpool, as 'a strange statistic' that 'sounds spurious' but nevertheless is 'trotted out locally with dead-pan confidence'. It reappeared in the same paper a month later, also trotted out with dead-pan confidence in a news feature on page 3, which is where I first encountered it. I had no reason to disbelieve the statistic, but I was curious about what it meant: What exactly was a 'Japanese computer game'? What does 'designed' mean in this context? So I e-mailed the *Guardian* journalists responsible for the piece I had read. Cheerfully they described the quote to me as 'absolute bollocks'. Evidently it had originated as a piece of PR from one of the chief computer game designers in Liverpool. It might just have had a grain of truth for one month in 1996, if that. It ought to have been corrected but journalists work at a rapid pace and the next deadline pushed it from their minds; however, they seemed genuinely delighted to have someone else, working to different imperatives, take up the task of correcting the record. The wheels of scholarship grind slow, sometimes painfully so; but this has its advantages. I had the time and the space to get better statistics from the software manufacturers' organisation: the British software industry ranks third in the world behind the US and Japan in the design of computer games – not so dramatic, though impressive enough. My research will not stop the factoid from flowing relentlessly onwards, but it might provide some interference. And at least I have unleashed the software manufacturers' better statistics from undeserved obscurity.

That is not very distinctively a historian's experience; it applies to academics of all kinds, and it makes the point that scholarship in general has important gatekeeping and quality-control functions in the information-rich society of the early twenty-first century. One hears often from government that we live in a 'knowledge economy' and that academics and teachers of all kinds have an important role to play in building up young people's skills to make the economy more productive and more competitive. But we live in a 'knowledge culture', too. A lot of what people do for fun, or for self-realisation or self-improvement, revolves around knowledge. The time and space that academics enjoy, and that society pays for, is crucial for the maintenance and development of that body of knowledge. The more commercial sectors of the knowledge culture – journalism, the mass media, the heritage industry – have come increasingly to rely upon academics for raising and policing standards that they cannot sustain on their own.

Historians are not alone in this role. But because people are today turning to history in growing numbers for their entertainment and self-development, and because historical knowledge *is* rather more arcane than some other knowledges rooted in the present, academic historians stand at an unusually significant and well-travelled crossroads between the university and the wider world. Consequently historians still have a central contribution to make to national life, long after national life has ceased to be organised centrally around the idea of the nation.

NOTES

I   The History Boom

1 David Starkey, 'The English Historian's Role and the
Place of History in English National Life', *The Historian*
(Autumn 2001), pp. 6–15.

II   Nationalist Origins (1800–1880)

1 Voltaire, 'On History: Advice to a Journalist', in F. Stern
(ed.), *The Varieties of History* (Cleveland, Ohio: World
Publishing Company, 1956), p. 36.
2 Ernest Renan, 'What is a Nation?', transl. Martin Thom,
in Homi K. Bhabha (ed.), *Nation And Narration*
(London; New York: Routledge, 1990), p. 11.
3 Augustin Thierry, 'First Letter on the History of France'

(1820), in Stern (ed.), *The Varieties of History*, p. 68.

4 Quoted in William Ruddick, 'Sir Walter Scott's Northumberland', in J. H. Alexander and David Hewitt (eds.), *Scott and His Influence* (Aberdeen: Association for Scottish Literary Studies, 1983), pp. 25–6.

5 Charles Robert Leslie, *Autobiographical Recollections*, 2 vols., ed. Tom Taylor (London: John Murray, 1860), vol. 2, p. 85.

6 [Herman Merivale], *Edinburgh Review* 74 (1841–2), pp. 434–5.

7 *Fraser's Magazine* 36 (1847), pp. 345–51.

8 Quoted in Roy Strong, *And When Did You Last See Your Father?: The Victorian Painter and British History* (London: Thames & Hudson, 1978), p. 31.

9 *Edinburgh Review* 48 (1828), p. 97.

10 Olive Anderson, 'The Political Uses of History in Mid Nineteenth-century England', *Past and Present* 36 (April 1967), pp. 87–105.

11 Quoted in J. W. Burrow, *A Liberal Descent: Victorian Historians and the English Past* (Cambridge: Cambridge University Press, 1981), p. 101.

12 John Richard Green, *Historical Studies* (London: Macmillan, 1903), pp. 105–6.

13 Green, *Historical Studies*, p. 67.

14 Helen Taylor (ed.), *Miscellaneous and Posthumous Works of Henry Thomas Buckle*, 3 vols. (London:

Longmans, Green, & Co., 1872), vol. 1, pp. xlii–xliii.

15 Quoted in Stefan Collini, Donald Winch and John
Burrow, *That Noble Science of Politics: A Study in
Nineteenth-century Intellectual History* (Cambridge:
Cambridge University Press, 1983), p. 192.

16 Leslie Stephen (ed.), *Letters of John Richard Green*
(London: Macmillan, 1901), p. 248.

17 J. R. Seeley, *The Expansion of England* (London:
Macmillan, 1883), pp. 237–8.

III Drifting Away (1880–1960)

1 Quoted in Christopher Parker, *The English Historical
Tradition since 1850* (Edinburgh: John Donald, 1990),
p. 88.

2 A. F. Pollard, 'The Growth of an Imperial Parliament',
History, A. s., 1 (1916–17), p. 131.

3 Herbert Butterfield, *The Whig Interpretation of History*
(London: G. Bell, 1931), p. 10.

4 From Galbraith's inaugural lecture, reprinted in V. H.
Galbraith, *An Introduction to the Study of History*
(London: C. A. Watts, 1964), p. 79.

5 Quoted in Robert Withington, *English Pageantry: An
Historical Outline*, 2 vols. (Cambridge, Mass.: Harvard
University Press, 1918–20), vol. 2, p. 195.

6 Ernest A. Fulton, 'History and the National Life', *History* 3 (1914), p. 64.

7 Eric C. Walker, 'History and the Unemployed Adolescent', *History*, n.s., 20 (1935–6), p. 139.

8 Quoted in Norman and Jeanne Mackenzie, *H. G. Wells* (New York: Simon & Schuster, 1973), p. 324.

9 Edgar Johnson, 'American Biography and the Modern World', *North American Review* 245 (1938), p. 369.

10 Earl of Crawford & Balcarres, 'History and the Plain Man', *History*, n.s., 23 (1938–9), pp. 297–8.

11 Quotations taken from the revised version, published as 'The Muse of History', in G. M. Trevelyan, *The Recreations of an Historian* (London: Thomas Nelson, 1919), pp. 11–60.

12 Quotations taken from reprint in F. Stern (ed.), *The Varieties of History* (Cleveland, Ohio: World Publishing Company, 1956), pp. 210–23.

13 G. M. Trevelyan, *Must England's Beauty Perish? A Plea on Behalf of the National Trust ...* (London: Faber & Gwyer, 1929), p. 19.

14 Trevelyan, *Recreations*, pp. 46, 52–3, 57.

15 Patrick Brindle, 'Mr Chips with Everything', *History Today* (June 1996), pp. 11–14.

16 J. W. Headlam, 'The Effect of the War on the Teaching of History', *History*, n.s., 3 (1918), p. 14.

17 Eric Fulton, 'History and the National Life', p. 63.

18 H. G. Wood, 'The Past – Incumbrance or Inspiration?',
   The Listener (10 August 1932), p. 196.

19 G. P. Gooch, 'History as a Training for Citizenship',
   Contemporary Review 137 (1930), pp. 347–52.

20 Walker, 'History and the Unemployed Adolescent',
   p. 139.

21 W. H. Burston, 'The Contribution of History to
   Education in Citizenship', *History*, n.s., 33 (1948),
   pp. 235–6.

22 Geoffrey Gorer, *Exploring English Character* (London:
   Cresset Press, 1955), pp. 286–7.

23 Burston, 'The Contribution of History to Education in
   Citizenship', p. 239.

24 L. B. Namier, 'History: Its Subject-Matter and Tasks',
   History Today, (March 1952), pp. 160–61.

25 E. H. Carr, *What Is History?*, 2nd edn, ed. R.W. Davies
   (Harmondsworth: Penguin, 1987), p. 66.

26 Carr, *What Is History?*, p. 171.

IV **Widening Horizons (1960–)**

1 Quoted in Kathleen Burk, *Troublemaker: The Life and
  History of A. J. P. Taylor* (New Haven, Conn.; London:
  Yale University Press, 2000), p. 391.

2 *Bookseller* (13 February 1965), p. 451.

3 Mary Price, 'History In Danger', *History* 53 (1968), pp. 342–7.

4 Richard Evans, 'How History Became Popular Again', *New Statesman* (12 February 2001), p. 27.

5 Peter Laslett, *The World We Have Lost*, 2nd edn (London: Methuen, 1971), p. 242.

6 G. R. Elton, *The Practice of History*, 2nd edn (Oxford: Blackwell, 2002), pp. 6, 16, 42–4.

7 Gordon Leff, 'The Past and the New', *The Listener* (10 April 1969), pp. 485–7.

8 R.W. Southern, 'The Historical Experience', *TLS* (24 June 1977), pp. 773–4.

9 H. R. Trevor-Roper, 'The Past and the Present: History and Sociology', *Past & Present* 42 (1969), p. 4.

10 Quotations from the version published in *The Listener* (12 March 1981), pp. 333–6.

11 Elton, *The Practice of History*, p. 4.

12 Quoted in Burk, *Troublemaker*, pp. 210–11.

13 John M. Roberts, 'History and Mass Media', *Manchester Memoirs* 126 (1986–7), pp. 48–60.

14 Angus Calder, *The Myth of the Blitz* (London: Jonathan Cape, 1991), p. xiv.

15 Robert Hewison, *The Heritage Industry: Britain in a Climate of Decline* (London: Methuen, 1987), p. 47.

16 Raphael Samuel, *Island Stories: Unravelling Britain* (London: Verso, 1998), pp. 214–23.

17 Caroline Sanderson, 'Their Lives in Our Hands',
   Bookseller (22 June 2001), p. 24.

V The Uses of History

1 Christopher Harvie, *No Gods and Precious Few Heroes:
  Twentieth-century Scotland*, 3rd edn (Edinburgh:
  Edinburgh University Press, 1998), p. 177.

ACKNOWLEDGEMENTS

I would like to thank first and foremost the Fellowship of the Royal Historical Society, whom I have served for the past four years as Honorary Secretary. Without the opportunities for learning and reflecting about history's place in society afforded me by this position I could not have written this book. I owe a special debt to Joy McCarthy, Peter Marshall and Jinty Nelson, whose wise and gentle guidance made my job easy and always pleasurable. Thanks to people like these three, the Society is no longer the inward-looking academics' club that it once was, but rather a vigorous advocate for a scholarly history with wide horizons and high ambitions.

Deborah Cohen and Mark Mazower read my chapters as they scrolled off my word processor and suggested invaluable amendments; the remaining blemishes are of course my own responsibility. A lot of people have helped me think about the uses of history over the past few years. Those who have made a direct contribution to the conclusions arrived at here (not necessarily by agreeing with them!) include Arthur Burns, Simon Ditchfield, Cyril Ehrlich, Eric Evans, Peter Furtado, Juliet Gardiner, Elizabeth Hallam Smith, Ludmilla Jordanova, Neil McKendrick, Charles Perry, Richard Rathbone, Paul Readman, Stella Tillyard and Giles Waterfield. Thanks also, for broadening my own horizons, to the many historic house curators I have met at the Attingham Summer Schools, to the staff at the Royal College of Art/Victoria & Albert Museum History of Design course, to a long parade of BBC radio researchers and producers, and to the history professionals at Wall-to-Wall Productions. London Guildhall University, Gonville and Caius College, and the University of Cambridge have, miraculously, paid me to be an historian. Peter Carson at Profile Books set me a tough deadline and then, along with Penny Daniel and Sally Holloway, made every effort to help me meet it. In my end is my beginning: David Cannadine asked me to write this book, and I hope he is satisfied with the results.

FURTHER READING

Much of this book is based upon historians' own statements – in books, lectures and journalism – about the value
of their craft. I have tried to indicate the key titles in the
text, or at least to give clues where they might be located.
Two excellent anthologies of such statements are Fritz Stern
(ed.), *The Varieties of History* (London: Thames & Hudson,
1956), which goes back to Voltaire, and John Tosh (ed.), *Historians on History* (Harlow: Pearson Education, 2000), fo-
cusing on the post-1945 period.

We now have some very good biographies of historians. My late lamented teacher John Clive wrote the definitive biography at least of the first half of Macaulay's life,
Macaulay: The Shaping of the Historian (New York: Knopf,
1973). The progress of Whig history from Macaulay
through Freeman, Stubbs and Green is traced in a master-
ful piece of intellectual history by John Burrow, *A Liberal*

Descent: Victorian Historians and the English Past (Cambridge: Cambridge University Press, 1981). For more on Green, see Anthony Brundage, *The People's Historian: John Richard Green and the Writing of History in Victorian England* (Westport, Conn.; London: Greenwood Press, 1994). Seeley is given thoughtful treatment in Deborah Wormell, *Sir John Seeley and the Uses of History* (Cambridge: Cambridge University Press, 1980). Stewart A. Weaver provides a dual biography of *The Hammonds: A Marriage in History* (Stanford, Calif.: Stanford University Press, 1997). The best of the bunch is David Cannadine on *G. M. Trevelyan: A Life in History* (London: HarperCollins, 1992), as readable as its subject. Maxine Berg's *A Woman in History: Eileen Power 1889–1940* (Cambridge: Cambridge University Press, 1996) adds several new dimensions to our understanding of academic history between the wars which my compressed account could not properly accommodate. A. J. P. Taylor has been biographised three times, by Robert Cole, Adam Sisman and, most thoroughly, by Kathleen Burk, as well as by himself in *A Personal History* (London: Hamish Hamilton, 1983). E. H. Carr is well-served by Jonathan Haslam, *The Vices of Integrity: E. H. Carr, 1892–1982* (London: Verso, 1999). Richard Evans has provided introductions to new editions of both Carr's *What is History?* (Basingstoke: Palgrave, 2001) and G. R. Elton's *The Practice of History* (Oxford: Blackwell, 2002) that put them nicely into the historiographical context of the 1960s.

There is no treatment of the professionalisation of history in Britain as comprehensive as that rendered for America by Peter Novick in *That Noble Dream: The 'Objectivity Question' and the American Historical Profession* (Cambridge: Cambridge University Press, 1988). Two more modest books which cover some of the same ground, but differ in interesting ways, are P. B. M. Blaas, *Continuity and Anachronism: Parliamentary and Constitutional Development in Whig Historiography and in the Anti-Whig Reaction Between 1890 and 1930* (The Hague; Boston: M. Nijhoff, 1978) and Christopher Parker, *The English Historical Tradition since 1850* (Edinburgh: John Donald, 1990).

On nationalist and popular history, a good starting point is Benedict Anderson, *Imagined Communities: Reflections on the Origin and Spread of Nationalism*, 2nd edn, (London: Verso, 1991), still the best treatment of why people come to feel like a nation and how they express that feeling. Eric Hobsbawm and Terence Ranger (eds.), *The Invention of Tradition* (Cambridge: Cambridge University Press, 1983), the book which invented that concept, remains the essential introduction. Stephen Bann's *The Clothing of Clio: A Study of the Representation of History in Nineteenth-century Britain and France* (Cambridge: Cambridge University Press, 1984) was a pioneering comparative study.

Roy Strong's *And When Did You Last See Your Father? The Victorian Painter and British History* (London: Thames & Hudson, 1978) was another trailblazer that deserves a new edition and a new audience. I broached some of the themes of chapter 2 of the present book in *The Fall and Rise of the Stately Home* (New Haven, Conn.; London: Yale University Press, 1997) and in an article, '"In the Olden Time": Romantic History and English National Identity, 1820–1850', in L. Brockliss & D. Eastwood (eds.), *A Union of Multiple Identities: The British Isles, c. 1750 – c. 1850* (Manchester: Manchester University Press, 1997). Our understanding of the origins of popular history in Britain has since been extended by Rosemary Mitchell, *Picturing the Past: English History in Text and Image 1830–1870* (Oxford; New York: Clarendon Press, 2000). History in schoolbooks is surveyed by Valerie E. Chancellor in *History for Their Masters: Opinion in the English History Textbook 1800–1914* (Bath: Adam & Dart, 1970). History in ordinary readers' lives is among the many subjects of Jonathan Rose's *The Intellectual Life of the British Working Classes* (New Haven, Conn.; London: Yale University Press, 2001). Julia Stapleton and Charles Perry are both working on books about popular history in the interwar period.

On the impact of mass communications, I have always been impressed – though not in all respects persuaded – by Neil Postman's *Amusing Ourselves To Death: Public Dis-*

course in the Age of Show Business (London: William Heinemann, 1986), which starts with the impact of the telegraph. A more measured and historical argument is made by D. L. LeMahieu in *A Culture for Democracy: Mass Communication and the Cultivated Mind in Britain Between the Wars* (Oxford: Clarendon Press, 1988). On the incredible late twentieth-century explosion in forms of historical consciousness, there is a fat catalogue of the varieties in David Lowenthal, *The Past is a Foreign Country* (Cambridge: Cambridge University Press, 1985). Raphael Samuel makes his own eccentric, stimulating, infuriating survey in *Theatres of Memory* (London; New York: Verso, 1994) and in a posthumous collection of essays, *Island Stories: Unravelling Britain* (London: Verso, 1998), which includes key interventions in the national curriculum debate. Stefan Collini's *English Pasts: Essays in History and Culture* (New York; Oxford: Oxford University Press, 1999) tenders some deliciously tart verdicts on the efforts of academic historians to popularise history.

INDEX